CONVENTION
SURVIVAL
TECHNIQUES

SURVIVAL SKILLS FOR SCHOLARS

Managing Editor: Peter Labella

Survival Skills for Scholars provides you, the professor or advanced graduate student working in a college or university setting, with practical suggestions for making the most of your academic career. These brief, readable guides will help you with skills that you are required to master as a college professor but may have never been taught in graduate school. Using hands-on, jargon-free advice and examples, forms, lists, and suggestions for additional resources, experts on different aspects of academic life give invaluable tips on managing the day-to-day tasks of academia—effectively and efficiently.

Volumes in This Series

SURVIVAL SKILLS FOR SCHOLARS

CONVENTION
SURVIVAL
TECHNIQUES

Practical Strategies for
Getting the Most Out of Your
Professional Association's Meetings

LOUIS R. FRANZINI
SUE ROSENBERG ZALK

SAGE Publications
International Educational and Professional Publisher
Thousand Oaks   London   New Delhi

For information:

SAGE Publications, Inc.
2455 Teller Road
Thousand Oaks, California 91320
E-mail: order@sagepub.com

SAGE Publications Ltd.
6 Bonhill Street
London EC2A 4PU
United Kingdom

SAGE Publications India Pvt. Ltd.
M-32 Market
Greater Kailash I
New Delhi 110 048 India

Printed in the United States of America

Library of Congress Cataloging-in-Publication Data

Franzini, Louis R., 1941-
    Convention survival techniques: Practical strategies for getting the most out of your professional association's meetings / by Louis Franzini and Sue Rosenberg Zalk.
        p. cm.—(Survival skills for scholars; v. 18)
    Includes index.
    ISBN 0-8039-7414-0 (acid-free paper).—ISBN 0-8039-7415-9 (pbk.: acid-free paper)
    1. Professional associations. 2. Congresses and conventions. 3. Professional socialization. I. Zalk, Sue Rosenberg. II. Title. III. Series.
    HD6496.5.F73 1997
    060—dc21   97-4701

This book is printed on acid-free paper.

97 98 99 00 01 02 03 10 9 8 7 6 5 4 3 2 1

Acquiring Editor:	Marquita Flemming
Editorial Assistant:	Frances Borghi
Production Editor:	Astrid Virding
Production Assistant:	Karen Wiley
Typesetter/Designer:	Danielle Dillahunt
Cover Designer:	Lesa Valdez
Print Buyer:	Anna Chin

To Jessica, my love,
for her constant support and unconditional love
—LRF

To my parents,
Ceal (1910-1990) and Sam Rosenberg
—SRZ

Contents

Preface

Why should you bother to attend your discipline's professional conventions? Isn't a convention just one big party? Aren't such meetings just convenient places for grad students to present their seminar papers? Why would professionals ever attend such meetings? How can you afford to take time off from your research or your teaching to go to a convention?

In this book we answer these common questions and attack some of the hidden assumptions behind them. We discuss the value and multiple advantages of attending professional conventions. We identify both the realistic concerns and the irrational fears that can sometimes serve to keep students and professionals from attending. Most important, we provide some strategies you can use to help you cope with those fears and concerns in order to get the most out of your association's annual conventions.

This book is a result of our accumulation of experiences and observations at many dozens of professional conventions and conferences over the course of our academic careers. Beginning in 1982 and each year thereafter, we have formally presented a convention orientation seminar at the annual meeting of the American Psychological Association at the invitation of its Board of Convention Affairs.

Our own students and various attendees at our convention seminars have provided many examples of ways to "survive" successfully at these meetings and have also pointed out some problems and pitfalls they have encountered, which we mention throughout the book. In the latter cases we try to make suggestions for dealing with such negative events, or, better yet, how to avoid them entirely when at all possible.

Undoubtedly, most readers will already be aware of some of the points we make here. All readers, however, certainly will acquire some new ideas, techniques, and strategies. Obviously, which particular ideas or strategies will be new will vary from person to person. There is definitely something of value in this book for everyone who is new to conventions. We stress the personal benefits of attending and participating, giving special attention to motivational factors and ways to overcome the barriers that can serve to deter you from becoming involved.

Discussing these issues in our seminars has always been fun. We try to retain that light, yet informative style here. Primarily, however, we want to be helpful to the advanced graduate students and new professionals who may be attending their first professional meetings. Our goal is for you not only to "survive" the convention, but to thrive there. When that happens, you will likely be inclined to return to future meetings, to participate actively in them, and to model these behaviors for your own future students.

Your own professional growth and the vitality of professional associations themselves are dependent on successful annual meetings. We sincerely hope that this book will contribute to both.

We thank our colleagues who have provided many useful illustrations, both positive and negative. We thank our past seminar audiences, who have been very complimentary and appreciative of our efforts (to be sure, a major social reward for speakers). Particular thanks go to our cartoonist, David Kelleher. Finally, we thank our editor, C. Deborah Laughton, for her encouragement and for inviting us to put on paper the ideas we have been promulgating over the years.

Attending a professional association's convention should be stimulating and rewarding, both professionally and socially. This is our main message. We truly believe that this volume will be a valuable vehicle to transport you to those rewards.

1 | Why Even Attend Conventions?

We have been conducting convention survival orientation sessions for a major professional association for well over a decade. The Board of Convention Affairs of the American Psychological Association sponsors our orientation because the board's members realize that first-timers can be overwhelmed by the association's massive annual meeting of 12,000 to 15,000 conventioneers. The newcomers to our sessions, of course, have already made the decision to attend the meeting; they come to our presentations in hopes that they will learn how to get the most they can out of the convention.

This guidebook represents our efforts to distill our most cogent suggestions into one practical, if not exciting, volume for interested students and newly minted academic professionals, in all disciplines, who may be hesitant to attend their professional associations' meetings. Their ambivalence can originate from reasonable concerns, irrational fears, and/or simple lack of information about what goes on at conventions and whether attending them is really worth their time.

First, attending your association's meetings *is* worth your time—of that we can confidently assure you. It is crucial, however, that you utilize your available time efficiently when you do attend. In this chapter we will highlight some of the obvious, and some not so obvious, benefits of attending conventions.

Second, some associations' meetings can definitely be large and intimidating. In these cases we would call your concerns reasonable, because it really can be difficult for a newcomer to navigate a large convention program and multiple meeting sites, and to understand the variety of forms of presentations scheduled, while also trying to identify the "hot," interesting speakers who will be presenting important new data in the field, all while possibly seeking a satisfying job for him- or herself at the same time. We address each of these elements of convention attendance in subsequent chapters.

In Chapter 11, we discuss the kinds of concerns and fears that often keep people away from professional association meetings and how you can overcome them. First, however, we want to accentuate the positive by describing the needs you can hope to fulfill by attending professional conventions.

Getting Your Needs Met at Meetings

We all have our different personal characteristics, unique abilities, and special needs. Similarly, at professional meetings the people attending most likely all have different needs and goals to be met. As Sigmund Freud taught us long ago, human behavior is multiply determined. Any single act can stem from a number of causes. A professional meeting serves many purposes, and the needs it fulfills will vary from person to person.

Based on previous surveys and our own interactions with hundreds of attendees at our past convention survival seminars, we have obtained extensive data on the many valid reasons people attend conventions. We categorize these varied needs into the following three areas: professionals' needs, students' needs, and social needs.

Professionals' Needs

We have found that there are five major professional reasons for attending annual meetings. These are, of course, most relevant for established professionals in a discipline, but they are also applicable to advanced students and beginning professionals. We don't believe it should be necessary for us to convince you of the value of these goals; that will be self-evident. Rather, we want to emphasize that attending your annual convention is an excellent way for you to get your professional needs met. In Chapter 2, we discuss the major strategies we recommend you use to go about fulfilling your professional needs efficiently and effectively.

Your first need as a professional is to *maintain and augment your currency in the field*. New discoveries, theories, and research data are typically presented at a discipline's annual meeting, long before they appear in its books or professional journals. Often these presentations are even newsworthy to the general public. Most associations maintain media rooms at their meetings, to facilitate coverage of presentations by the print and electronic news media. Presumably, as a professional, you will be interested in the latest developments that are being presented for nonlaypersons as well. In brief, to stay up-to-date in your field, you *must* attend your association's annual meetings.

Arthur Nezu, editor of *the Behavior Therapist*, recently described his own reasons for continuing to attend professional conventions even though he is a senior member in his field, a department chair, and an associate dean. Among the obvious benefits of opportunities for new learning and intellectual growth, Dr. Nezu also especially values the chance to see the fruits of his labor, the influence he has had on his students and colleagues in their research and clinical work. Even when conducting workshops, he admits, he gains a tremendous amount from his audiences as well.

We often hear transparent excuses and rationalizations from professionals explaining why they do not attend meetings. For example, "I am too busy right now with my research [or writing, or grant preparations, or reading, or grading exams, or whatever]." Or, "I can read the papers later in the journals." Or, "The meetings are boring." Or, "I can't afford it." Or, much less often admitted, "I am intimidated by large meetings with many people." Or, "I get too anxious speaking to groups in public." Throughout this book we will address such concerns and fears. We believe that professionals who have such concerns and fears are those who need the meetings most. Meanwhile, what behaviors (and fears) are they modeling for their students?

To write and then submit a grant proposal that will be competitive with those of other experts in the field, a professional must be aware of the most current theories and empirical data in his or her area. Conventions feature research updates in one form or another by the key players in the field. It is vital that anyone hoping to write a successful grant proposal hear those presentations and incorporate any relevant information in the proposal. Getting to know the key players in your discipline is a critical form of social networking that has direct payoffs in your professional life. For instance, those same key players are often part of granting agencies' peer review panels. We would not suggest, of course, that panel members are more likely to rank proposals just a little higher (or more) when the proposals have been submitted by professional friends, but we would argue that it certainly does not hurt. In a very important sense, professionals who are grant seekers cannot afford not to go to their conventions.

Perhaps the most important reason for teaching professionals in any discipline to attend and participate actively in their annual conventions is that this activity provides excellent role modeling for the students who are the association's future professionals. Many a graduate student has told us, "My mentor does not attend conventions; she says they are unimportant." This is not good mentoring.

When students observe their valued mentors presenting, responding to questions or critiques, and interacting informally with fellow professionals and students at professional meetings, they learn how productive and active professionals in the field should behave. Modeling, especially by high-prestige models, is without question an extraordinarily effective teaching tool.

The second need you have as a professional is to be able *to present your own work in a "safe" environment*; attendance at an annual meeting presents you with a valuable opportunity to do so. Bringing your recent projects to the attention of fellow professionals gives you an incentive to organize the material for presentation, which then becomes a vehicle through which you can receive reasoned feedback and constructive criticism on your work. You can then accept any appropriate recommendations for changes, such as different ways to organize or analyze the data, obtain differing perspectives for interpretation, or even identify additional target participants for inclusion. Changes made as a function of this preliminary presentation to colleagues at the meeting can be invaluable in strengthening your work. This process can smooth your transition to presenting projects in a professional journal format.

Another major benefit of presenting your work at a professional convention is that it strengthens your curriculum vita or résumé. Presentations at professional meetings are generally important for promotion and can be a strong advantage when you are seeking employment. Participation in presentations demonstrates that you are professionally active and productive. This is particularly true for new professionals, who are not likely to have a plethora of publications; a record of presenting at professional meetings shows "promise." Additionally, presenting your work to others in your field is excellent experience for you, if your field is one in which lectures and presentations will be an integral part of your working life.

The third professional need you can meet by attending conventions is your need to *network with colleagues*. This advantage follows directly from the preceding need, but it is worthy of mention on its own. *Networking* is the current term used to refer to the development of contacts and actual friendships with other members of one's profession. Such contacts represent important human resources that you can use (in the best sense of the term) and rely upon for advice, advance information, support when you run for office or seek other official involvement in the association, and accrual of all the advantages of informal social recognition in the field.

Networking provides you with opportunities to meet others doing work in your area and, perhaps, to develop collaborative projects or ongoing dialogues. It also facilitates your meeting "big names" in your field who can provide you with direction or contacts to advance your career development. Networking can help you gain valuable professional visibility for the future.

Fourth, the professional meeting is the ideal forum for fulfilling professionals' needs in the areas of *job seeking and recruiting*. Often meetings provide formal placement services that offer all the available information on positions open and facilitate contacts between job seekers and recruiters.

Tip: If you are seeking a job or recruiting for one, we recommend that you contact the association several months prior to the meeting dates in order to list your position or your availability for a position in the convention's printed booklet. Those who wait until they get to the meeting to list such information usually become part of a supplementary publication, which may not get as wide a distribution as the originally prepared booklet listing various employment announcements. Most associations charge modest fees to list available positions, but may not charge at all or may charge lesser fees to publish individuals' announcements of their availability. Of course, networking also functions as an invaluable aid to job seeking and recruiting. Despite modern legal requirements for "open" processes in matching positions with applicants, the value of early informal contacts remains unquestioned.

Finally, the annual meeting fills the professional's need to *learn of new publications and publishing opportunities*. Many major publishing houses and manufacturers of technical equipment rent space in conventions' exhibit areas to promote their latest books and products. See Chapter 8 for more detailed observations and recommendations concerning this standard feature of conventions.

Publishers' senior editors are likely to be present at many associations' national meetings, and they are always pleased to discuss with you any writing projects you have planned (at least during working hours). If, even as an advanced graduate student, you are teaching basic courses, you can offer to review textbooks for publishers in those areas. For this service, publishers pay modest fees (typically $100 to $300, depending on the extent of their need for information from you). Such a consulting relationship can blossom eventually into a publisher-author relationship. Your very presence at your association's meeting identifies you as an active, current, and inquisitive participant in the field, and that is the kind of author publishers are seeking (along with the abilities to write coherent sentences and to use a spell checker occasionally).

Students' Needs

In addition to some overlap with the professional needs described above, the annual national convention can meet a number of needs unique to those who are new or prospective students in the field.

Motivated and able undergraduate students can *research master's and doctoral programs* at annual meetings in ways not available to them in the printed program brochures. If you are a prospective student, you may be able to learn what particular programs are really like by talking with students already studying in programs at those universities, and even with faculty at those universities. For example, are the resources such as labs and libraries as well equipped as they are described in program brochures? What are the internship and practicum realities and availabilities? What about intangibles such as student and faculty morale? The politics of the department? Possible problems with harassment or other exploitative practices? What are the success records of recent graduates? Are there quality mentoring experiences available? Are they available for people "like you"—that is, of your gender, race, sexual orientation, interest areas, and so on?

Many of these topics are indeed sensitive, so there is always a chance that the people you speak with may have vested interests or their own axes to grind. It is important to remember those qualifiers as you interpret your "interview data." On the other hand, you can often obtain information in this informal manner that will be more valuable to you than your adviser's weight in precious metals.

Students who attend associations' annual meetings are demonstrating initial *professional visibility*. Such students, who understand and welcome the appropriate professional role, impress faculty very positively, and those same faculty are the people who will review the students' subsequent applications for admission to graduate programs. Similarly, those employers who are at meetings to recruit prospects for available jobs will note and remember students who are already professionally involved in associations. A student's presentation of a paper or poster or participation in a symposium highlights that student's demonstrated professionalism. Many doctoral programs, as well as jobs, are so highly competitive that such professional activities have become practically mandatory for successful applicants.

The annual meeting permits advanced students to *survey the job market,* sometimes a year or two before they must actually step into those uncertain waters. A student's first professional job is sometimes given insufficient attention by graduate school mentors who simply would like to get the student "placed" somewhere. In fact, that first job has many implications for the direction and ultimate level of the student's lifetime career. It is crucial to remember that not all entry-level jobs are alike, and there are many vital dimensions to consider beyond base salary and pension plans. For example, is the first work setting an academic institution or an applied or service delivery setting? If an academic institution, is it a small teaching college or a research-oriented major university? Geographically, will the first job be in a large urban environment or a small-town or rural location? Is it a hard- or soft-money job (i.e., dependent upon grant funding)? All of these dimensions and decisions are germane to the student's future career possibilities. Conventions include attendees from all these different kinds of settings (and more). Students can easily obtain invaluable information from these persons that will promote their making more fully informed choices when they are ready to seek their first professional positions.

Finally, most professional associations include *graduate student organizations* with which students can connect. These groups vary widely in their activism and effectiveness. Ordinarily, they are worthwhile and highly beneficial to fellow graduate students because they share many of the same goals of the working professionals in the field as well as the convention survival goals we are stressing here. For example, some such organizations are actively political and may lobby as larger groups for the "rights" of graduate students in the field. Such rights might include health benefits for teaching and research assistants at universities, protections from harassment at work and in the classroom, guarantees against discrimination for any of the many possible biases they might encounter (e.g., race, ethnicity, gender, age, physical status, sexual orientation, religion, national origin of ancestry, positive HIV status, mental disability), and other issues of importance to university graduate students.

Social Needs

Let's be candid and clear about the value of fulfilling social needs at an annual convention (the IRS is not listening). Meeting old friends from graduate school and colleagues from other institutions and other areas of the country and the world is truly a major benefit of attending your association's meeting. This can be part of professional networking, of course, but it is also a legitimate tax-deductible opportunity to renew personal friendships. Old friends are likely to introduce you to others they may be talking with, and your social and professional network expands accordingly. Then the members of that group become people with whom you can consider renewing contact at the next meeting. In Chapter 7, we discuss in much greater detail a variety of strategies for meeting your social needs in the convention setting.

Extraconvention Opportunities

Each year, most American professional associations hold their major meetings in different cities in the United States or Canada. You should not ignore the many valuable opportunities available for recreation, dining, and typical tourism that accompany the convention setting itself. It can be fun to explore a new city, master its subway system, hear a concert, see a play, visit an art gallery or zoo, or try a new restaurant with someone interesting whom you have just met at a paper session or a social hour at the convention.

In attending conventions, you will undoubtedly be visiting some cities that you would otherwise have no particular reason to see. Avail yourself of all the special features of each city. Yes, that could mean actually visiting the Statue of Liberty in New York City, if you never have, or going to Universal Studios in Los Angeles. Also, every city features special restaurants, ethnic and otherwise, that are not available anywhere else. Our main caveat is that you should schedule your tourist and recreation activities around ongoing convention presentations. If possible, it may be wise to get to the convention city a day or two prior to the start of the meeting itself, or to stay on a bit longer after the meeting ends.

Summary

We all attend conventions for a variety of reasons, professional and social, all legitimate. As both professionals and students, we have both unique and overlapping needs that can be met at conventions, with proper planning. Conventions can and should be informative, professionally stimulating, vocationally helpful, and socially enjoyable. We are confident that by following the advice in this book, you will be well on your way not only to surviving a convention but to capitalizing on the many possible rewards available to you there. That, in turn, helps us fulfill our goals. Everyone gains!

2 | General Strategies for Convention Survival

Achieving happiness in life, gaining success at work, and finding harmony in personal relationships are all facilitated by prior preparation and practice. Lo and behold, the same is true for convention survival! Getting the most out of your professional association's annual meeting is intimately related to your proper preparation for the function. You can and should begin preparing at least a few weeks before the convention actually convenes.

In this chapter we review some general tactics you can use to prepare for a convention and survive it. In later chapters we address related topics more specifically. We guarantee that with some guidance and a dash of inspiration, the chances of your having a rewarding experience will go up dramatically. You will learn not only to survive but to succeed at conventions.

The Role of Preparation

Obtain the official convention program early, if at all possible. Some associations will send out programs several weeks in advance of meeting dates, if you preregister. Preregistering almost always results in financial savings for you as well.

Preparation is the single most important variable for ensuring a successful and rewarding convention experience. It is hard to overemphasize the role of preparation because it affects all other important areas of convention attendance. Preparation can save you money in transportation, hotel, dining, and recreation costs (see Chapter 9 for details). Preparation can save you valuable time, by giving you prior familiarity with the planned program and how to navigate the convention halls and local city streets efficiently (see Chapter 3 for tips on mastering the convention program book). Preparation can help you meet your social needs; if you plan in advance, you can contact friends and colleagues from other cities about whether they will also be going to the meeting and, if so, where to contact them (see Chapter 7 for some specific strategies regarding social matters and Chapter 10 for effective convention communication techniques). Preparation can also help you be ready to make further plans; for example, when you meet new people at the convention, you can make plans to renew your friendships at the next one.

Assertiveness and Social Skills

We highly recommend the convention setting as an excellent place for you to practice and implement your assertiveness and social skills. No other psychological variables are as important as these to your convention success. Perhaps you have participated in assertiveness seminars at some point in the past, or have read some of the popular books on the topic. Certainly you are likely to be familiar with some of the basic concepts of assertiveness.

When you are unassertive in acting to get your needs met at a convention, just as in other life situations, you are very likely to end up feeling lonely and depressed. Basic social skills such as smiling, even at strangers, and starting up conversations with potentially interesting people can lead to many reward-ing interactions and even permanent friendships.

We have known both students and colleagues who frantic-ally rush into meetings, register, give their papers or present their posters, and then immediately rush back home to their labs or offices. Why? We have found that it is extreme lack of comfort in new social situations, often accompanied by unrea-sonable fears, that usually prevents these people from attend-ing or enjoying conventions. If they do attend, they tend to spend most of their time alone and generally end up having aversive experiences, which, of course, results in their failure to attend future meetings. They may even proceed to promote negative reviews of conventions in general to their colleagues and students, disguising the real reasons that underlie their unpleasant experiences. There is no need for this to happen. Our whole purpose here is to show you how to survive and succeed at professional conventions.

Assertiveness very simply means being aware of your per-sonal rights and freedom to express your opinions, wishes, and feelings, while simultaneously taking the rights of others into account. It means doing what you want to do and say and not doing or saying what you do not want to.

We use the term *social skills* here primarily to refer to conver-sation skills. How does one initiate, maintain, and terminate a conversation when one wishes? Actually, these are three differ-ent skills. Sometimes a person can be good at just one or two of these aspects of conversation, but not the third. For example, how often have you heard an otherwise verbally skilled person complain that some friend or relative just kept him or her on the phone endlessly and wouldn't stop talking, when this per-son had other things to do or was just tired of talking?

Professional conventions are great places for you to apply your assertiveness and conversation skills. Attendees by defini-tion are out of their familiar and comfortable social environ-ments. They must call upon a variety of social skills that they do not ordinarily need, and they may feel less confident than usual in such settings. Your social skills and assertiveness are the keys

"I HAVEN'T ACTUALLY HEARD ANY PAPERS YET...I'M PRACTISING MY ASSERTIVENESS SKILLS."

that will unlock the secrets of getting your needs (professional, vocational, academic, and social) met with ease—guaranteed!

Conventioneers are always issued name badges upon registration. These badges usually also indicate the wearers' hometowns or professional affiliations. At the American Psychological Association's annual meetings, attendees also have other optional additions for their name badges. For example, adhesive stickers with the number 1 on them are available for first-time convention attendees to place on their badges. These identify the wearers as newcomers, so that other psychologists, if they are socially motivated to be helpful, can volunteer assistance and warmly welcome them. Of course not every first-timer, especially the unassertive, chooses to apply this sticker, which is exactly the problem. Other optional color-coded stickers available to add to name badges at APA meetings are those intended to signify that wearers are either seeking jobs or recruiting for jobs. Via these sticker communication codes, it is possible for job matches to occur (eventually), if the seekers and recruiters seize the opportunity to speak about their stickers.

Some convention badges may have colorful ribbons attached. These do not ordinarily connote that the wearers have won any special prizes or been wounded at previous conventions. Rather, the ribbons indicate that the persons wearing them are officers or past officers of the association or that they are workshop presenters or invited speakers at the current meeting. Usually, there is lettering on such ribbons that will reveal their meaning. Obviously, the wearers of such ribbons are proud to display them, and they would surely respond positively to your taking notice of them with a positive comment.

The identifying information and any added stickers or ribbons on attendees' name badges can be an ideal starting point for initiating conversation. It is usually easy to note a person's institution or hometown and then ask if he or she knows another person you may know there. Or if you are seeking data on graduate programs at the person's institution, you could readily introduce that topic. At a convention you do not need a formal introduction to say hello to anyone or to ask for a point of information related to the meeting. If the reception is cordial and encouraging, you may choose to advance the discussion by gradually introducing social topics. And if that effort is successful, the conversational horizons and relationship possibilities become unlimited.

The point is, simply, Speak up! Ask a question. Give a compliment. Say "hi." Ask where a certain meeting room is located in the hotel or convention center. Comment on the speaker or the topic or the size of the room, its temperature, or anything appropriate to the setting. Your comment does not have to be made up; it is better if you make an observation that is genuine and true for you. There is no need to be false or deceptive. Most important, just be yourself.

Say something funny, especially if you are good at spontaneous humor that is socially appropriate. We do not mean you should tell a formal joke. Making a witty comment or noting some peculiarity at the convention will do just fine. Be clear that your remarks are lighthearted by using a humorous tone. It is wise to avoid complaining and sarcasm. Most people don't find those styles very appealing in a new friend. Above all, make your comments or ask your questions in a polite, friendly fashion with an accompanying *smile*. This approach nearly always works.

Poster sessions, by definition (see Chapter 4 for a more detailed description), are designed to promote informal interaction between the presenter and the attendees. This setting then dictates the appropriateness of your initiating conversation, which will usually be related to the topic of the presenter's poster, at least initially. It is unwise to move on to proffering a dinner invitation too quickly, but such is certainly not an unreasonable outcome from an enjoyable polite conversation.

Barriers to Behaving Assertively

Watch out for self-statements (some nonpsychologists would refer to these as your thoughts) that could deter you from using your assertive conversational skills. For example, some unassertive convention-goers who reflect on their convention experiences as lonely or boring typically have been telling themselves, "My question [or comment] isn't very important"; "He [or she] is too important for me to approach [or ask a question of]"; "I will speak only if she [or he] speaks to me first"; "I will sound stupid if I ask that question [or make that comment]"; "I don't know anyone here"; "I'm too anxious to say hello to a stranger"; "I'll make a fool of myself"; "I'll stutter and stammer [or belch or lose bowel control]."

All such negative self-statements lower the chances that an individual will actually initiate any conversation at a meeting. These kinds of statements also reflect a punishing attitude toward the self, as if the person is "not worthy" of attention or having his or her inquiries answered. In mild cases, such people experience very limited social contacts and tend to describe their personal lives as dull and lonely. In more severe cases, they could become prone to depression and pessimism, both of which end up making them even less attractive to others as social conversation partners. In extreme cases, we would recommend professional therapeutic attention; most readers, however, surely do not suffer to this extent. We are simply trying to stimulate you to display the abilities you probably already possess to a large degree.

We are assuming that our gentle urging and some early successes out in the field will be sufficient to motivate you to speak up and ask for what you want in the social setting of the convention. For any more extreme inhibitions or even full-fledged clinical social phobias, consultation with a qualified therapist would be necessary.

No one at a convention is going to be offended by your courteous inquiries or polite small talk. Many other attendees will be experiencing the same anxieties or concerns that you are. In fact, all conventioneers wonder about such things as how to find a place to sit down to rest and read the program, and how to learn where a good place for lunch might be. Why not share your concerns or questions with someone? Even where the nearest restrooms, public phones, or cold water fountains are located can be very valuable information to know and to share. People who share are people who care!

As the Nike ads urge us, "Just do it!" Any given conversational interaction will not necessarily lead to a love connection or even a particularly interesting discussion. It might or it might not—it doesn't really matter. If no great connection is made, you have at least gotten some practice in assertiveness and social skills, and you probably have also gotten your initial question answered. You will have learned something, and that, after all, is one of the main reasons you are even attending the meeting—to learn. And the next time, who knows?

Special Considerations

Most professional associations are very cognizant of the need to avoid even the appearance of discrimination against any members or prospective members based on ethnicity, religion, gender, sexual orientation, or physical abilities. Of course, problem instances may still conceivably occur, albeit very infrequently, in dining, in housing, or even in the hotel lounge regarding who may dance with whom.

Given our legal protections against discrimination in the United States, and the practice of basic social courtesies, these issues should not arise. However, if discriminatory actions do occur, they should not be tolerated; convention officials, such as the overall coordinator or manager of the meeting for the association, should be promptly informed. If the matter seems to be the direct responsibility of the hotel or convention center, officials of that organization should be contacted immediately as well. It is assertive, and certainly not aggressive, to do so.

Summary

Once you are convinced that you should attend an annual convention, you can practically guarantee a successful meeting for yourself by following our three key general recommendations: Prepare thoroughly for travel to the convention city, prepare by mastering the convention program itself and planning your schedule with flexibility, and use your assertiveness and social skills to obtain any desired information and to meet new and interesting people.

In the chapters that follow, we detail specific techniques that can help you achieve your personal and professional goals at a convention. Your goal, and our goal for you, is not just survival, but real success at the meeting on all those dimensions that are most important to you. When it all works for you, you will return for more meetings and will surely encourage your own students and colleagues to attend also.

3 | Mastering the Convention Program

The convention program is a book that lists all the scheduled presentations at the meeting plus assorted other kinds of information of value for attendees. For large associations, the program book can be the size of a telephone book for a moderate-sized city—that is, it may comprise several hundred pages. A program that size can indeed be intimidating and formidable. Your success in understanding and using the convention program to navigate the many options available is directly related to your getting the most out of your convention.

We are aware of at least one professional association's convention book that contains an informative tip sheet on the inside cover on "how to read the program." Such a feature is a valuable aid, but unfortunately most programs leave you entirely on your own to make the best of figuring them out. That is why we are including this chapter. If your program is the combination lock that can open the many treasures to be found at the meeting, this chapter can be your guide to discovering the right combination.

Programs for different associations' annual meetings vary in their details and specifics. Some of the points we mention below may apply to your group's program; some may not. Our guidelines are necessarily general; they are relevant to just some, if not all, convention programs. We try to be as inclusive as possible, in order to cover most of the convention program features you may encounter.

The Importance of Preparation

When you preregister for a meeting, your professional association often will send you the convention program several weeks in advance of the meeting dates. This is the optimum situation. You can then take the requisite time to study the program in great detail and to plan your time for each day. When planning your day, of course, you need to remember that your schedule should remain just a rough outline, with enough built-in flexibility to accommodate last-minute changes as new opportunities present themselves. Generally, your only rigid time plans will concern your appearance at your own presentations and any personal or professional appointments set by others.

The single best piece of advice we can offer on mastering the program is that you review the program well in advance and sketch out each day's schedule for yourself. The more you can accomplish at home, prior to the time pressures you will experience at the meeting itself, the more efficient and productive your actual convention time will be. For example, some very large associations hold their meetings simultaneously at a variety of hotels and convention centers in a given city. At such a meeting, in addition to planning what you would like to attend and when, you will have to build in transit time from hotel to hotel. That could mean just 5 minutes to walk across the street in Washington, D.C., to a half hour or more to walk or take a cab some distance in New York City. It may be advisable for you to try to stay an entire morning or afternoon in the same facility, to avoid losing valuable time in transit. For this reason, convention program schedulers often try to offer similar topics and special interest group sessions in the same facilities on the same days.

Tip: You can always write to a presenter for a reprint of any paper or poster session presentation that you miss because of schedule conflicts (see Chapter 5 for some suggestions on requesting papers). Given that copies of presentations made at symposia and panel discussions are rarely available upon request, it may be wisest for you to try to attend these kinds of presentations "live." Incidentally, these less formal discussion sessions by well-known experts in the discipline may well be more lively, unrehearsed, and stimulating than any data-oriented research reports. We recommend you give them special attention in your planning for those reasons alone.

Structure of the Program Book

The first few pages of the program typically feature general information about the convention: hotel names and phone numbers, location of registration desks, job placement services area and exhibits hall, costs of registration for various member and nonmember categories, special services and events, and maps of all the floors of the hotel or convention center where meeting rooms are. It is of little help to know that you want to attend a session at 2 p.m. Friday in the Maricopa Room if you do not know the hotel or floor within the hotel where that room is located. Being familiar with the names of the rooms and floors of the various convention hotels will save you considerable time at the actual convention.

Tip: The print on hotel floor plans and city maps can be extremely small; you may want to carry a pocket-sized magnifying glass with you to avoid the annoyance of eyestrain you may suffer in reading them. (Difficulty in reading the tiny print is *not* necessarily a matter of increasing age. Some print really is too small.)

Most conventions include media rooms, where members of the electronic or print news media can obtain copies of papers and other pertinent information on the speakers and their topics. Usually there is also a speaker-ready room for presenters, where they can review their slides and check out projector carousels if needed. This room may include copy, fax, and tape machines to facilitate preparations for presentations. We know of at least one major professional association that now photocopies and sells each paper presented, for those who could not hear particular papers or who would like permanent written copies. Current retail price is $1.50 per paper. The locations of these special facilities are usually noted in the front of the convention program book.

Many books also give some basic data on availability and modes of local transportation, standard costs of transportation to and from the major airports and rail stations, and special local recreation and tourist information (e.g., nearby restaurants, sightseeing opportunities, sporting events scheduled, local shopping opportunities, and any special seasonal attractions in town at that time).

Most meetings, even relatively small ones, offer exhibit areas where vendors rent space to display books and other products of interest to the members of the discipline. When there are many exhibitors, each is usually assigned a booth number, and a map of the area, showing exhibiting companies by booth numbers, may be provided in the program book—this can be very helpful for locating a particular company quickly. Some programs give brief descriptions of all exhibiting companies, along with their office addresses and phone numbers. Associations very much need the participation of exhibitors to help defray the costs of putting on their conventions. In turn, the exhibitors gain a captive audience of conventioneers, all of whom by definition share common interest in the discipline. (See Chapter 8 for our tips on "surfing the exhibits.")

A good convention program summarizes special features of the meeting in the front of the book. If there will be one or more themes for the topics of the meeting, they are announced and defined here. Also, information relevant to those seeking continuing education credits is described. Most professions are now requiring documentation of members' continuing education through attendance at workshops or convention sessions, or through presenting at meetings. These rules and guidelines are usually noted in the program.

Finally, special preconvention and postconvention institutes or travel opportunities, if scheduled, are ordinarily mentioned in the front of the program. Such institutes may charge additional fees over the regular convention registration. The advantages of attending them are that they usually feature the giants of the profession in intensive, longer formats. Your own participation in such institutes can give you important specialized training with the biggest names in your business. This can be a convenient and rewarding way to meet your educational requirements while on a tax-deductible combination professional function/vacation.

Large conventions extend over a number of days. Programs are organized on a day-by-day basis, sometimes with convenient printed tabs for each day. You can highlight the sessions each day that are of greatest interest to you. **Tip:** You might want to use different colored highlighters to prioritize different topics of interest as you review the available topics of each day. You will then easily be able to follow your well-considered plan, while at the same time remaining flexible to change given new information that may emerge on site. For example, you may meet someone who asks if you would like to accompany him or her to a particular session that you had not previously considered. Occasionally, due to illness or other last-minute changes, a given session is canceled or a new and interesting one added too late to be included in the printed program. In sum, preview the program, plan your schedule, check out the changes, and stay flexible.

The program's index of participants lists all the authors of papers and poster, symposium, and panel presenters scheduled for the convention, sometimes with their professional addresses. *Caution:* Not all of these individuals will actually be present for the meeting. It is customary and expected that at least the first author of multiply authored presentations will be physically present. Sometimes all the authors are there; sometimes not. The index is a useful tool for you to use in following a particular individual's latest work or to contact someone who will be presenting. You can be reasonably sure that an individual will be at his or her own scheduled session. If your interest is to meet one of a paper's junior authors, that person could be there, or at least you likely could get a message to him or her by speaking to the actual presenter.

The index of participants lists each presenter's last name and first name (or initials) and a number. *Caution:* Sometimes this number refers to the page number within the program that describes the presentation title and format, but other times the number refers to the session number in the program. We find the latter method somewhat less helpful because a large poster session, for example, could contain a list of 50 or more papers with multiple authors and affiliations described over several pages. Looking for a particular individual among them could take an unnecessarily great amount of time. It can be cumbersome to have to scan numerous pages of presentations to find the person you particularly would like to see. It is more convenient for readers when the program provides the session numbers for small paper sessions and symposia.

The index of participants sometimes includes the professional addresses of the presenters as well as their names; this can be very helpful if you would like to write to particular individuals later to request reprints or to discuss their research or your own work in some detail. It is often socially unwise to get into very specific or complicated technical matters in conversation with a presenter immediately after he or she has presented. It can be flattering to the presenter, but it can be an imposition to expect a very involved research discussion in that setting. Obtaining an office address (or phone number) from the speaker directly or from the index will allow you to pursue the matter later, when it is likely more convenient for both of you.

Some meetings' programs feature subject indexes as well. However, we have found that the topics in such indexes tend to be so broad and general that they are often of little practical use. Typically a given topic will have dozens of related presentation numbers or pages given. Check for a subject index, but be prepared for a rather laborious search through the program if you try to use it.

The program books for relatively small meetings are often able to include a small abstract or summary of each presentation. This information can be extremely useful in allowing you to determine whether, in fact, a topic is in your interest area and gives a brief hint of what was studied and learned in the project to be discussed. Regional meetings and smaller group conferences are most likely to have the program space luxuries to print such overviews of presentations.

Commercial audiotaping companies often contract to tape and then sell certain key presentations at a meeting. These tapes can be purchased shortly after the presentations taped, throughout the meeting duration and for a reasonable time thereafter. Some programs note which sessions are planned to be taped by including a printed graphic of a cassette tape or some other symbol next to the listings for those sessions. Incidentally, any speaker who is being taped must give permission to the company doing the recording. In return, the speaker may receive a free copy of the presentation, but no other royalty is provided.

If your association is sufficiently large, it likely includes a number of divisions that reflect members' subareas of interests. When that is the case, sessions listed in the program may be noted as being sponsored by one or more of those divisions. Thus attendees can note which sessions will cover their own particular interest areas as they scan the full program to prepare their personal schedules. Sometimes, the sessions are cross-referenced with division-sponsored or division-relevant meetings.

Predicting Popular Presenters

Every association has certain members who are very well known for their expertise and for their dynamic presentations. Naturally, these persons will attract large audiences when they speak at a meeting. Sometimes convention planners fail to account for this phenomenon and schedule all presenters in similar rooms. When that happens, famous people are often assigned to present in tiny meeting rooms, while interested listeners sit all over the floor and spill out into the hall, straining to see and hear. Everyone is uncomfortable, and many people are denied the opportunity to enjoy a presentation by one of the leaders of the field.

You cannot make the room assignments for the speakers, but you can plan your own schedule to allow for a little earlier arrival at the sessions given by the "stars" of the profession. Getting there a little early is worth it and wise to assure yourself of getting in on the latest and the best.

Naturally, we cannot provide you with the specific names of the stars of your discipline. Those names will change over the years as new stars are born, old ones fade, and the politics of the profession change. In all humility, we admit that seats usually remain available throughout our own presentations (although twice we have been scheduled in rooms that were too small—it was most gratifying!)

Summary

Our best advice to you is this: Become very familiar with the program book *before* you leave home for the convention itself. A second-best option is to review the program during your long travel time to the convention city. At the meeting, carrying the program with you to lunch or on the street will identify you to fellow conventioneers and itself could serve as a conversational starting point. (See Chapter 7 for other useful tips on getting your social needs met.) Careful preparation, including planning how you will spend your professional and social time, is the absolute best way to survive and thrive at a convention.

4 | Program Formats

Their Differences and You

As the many academic disciplines have become more complex, perhaps inevitably, convention formats have also become more complex and intimidating. Whereas some of these formats are distinctly different, others can appear identical to the attending audience. The differences are sometimes subtle. More often, however, it is the intention, rather than the reality, that differs.

Those conventions with thick convention programs offer a plethora of different format headings. Some, such as symposia and workshops, are familiar concepts to most of us. Others, like poster sessions and conversation hours, are the creative by-products of individual convention planners. To their creators (lowercase *c*), the terms applied to these formats are designed to reflect the gist of what takes place in these sessions. Once the terms are chosen, however, they are often assumed to have universal meaning. Convention planners rarely stop to question whether new conventioneers have even the slightest idea of what to expect in any given session. In fact, the impression most newcomers have is that everyone else knows the distinctions among formats. As a result, few people at our convention orientation session ever question the differences, although when we ask them if they know the distinctions between terms, the majority say they don't.

Sessions: The Umbrella Term

Regardless of specific formats, at many conventions all the different components of the meeting are generically referred to as *sessions*. This makes life easier when it comes to communicating and negotiating your schedule, for example, to make time to meet with a friend: "I am attending a one o'clock session on sleep disorders after lunch, are you free at two?" "There's an interesting session on maze-solving skills in fatherless rats at three o'clock. Want to meet there?"

Session is the term used when there is no need to refer to the specific format. However, you might want to be more exact to make an explanatory point. For example, "I want to attend the two o'clock poster session on nontraditional parenting; come along!" (Specifying the format in this context implicitly means you and your companion will be able to talk at the same time.) Or, "I have a business meeting I must attend" (meaning that this is not an intellectual activity but rather an obligation or desire because of your involvement or interest in a particular subgroup or division).

Although referring to *sessions* works in almost all circumstances, it is useful to understand the distinctions among convention presentation formats. It will be helpful for you to know what to expect and what may be expected of you.

Presentation Formats

The meanings of the terms used to describe presentation formats may vary slightly from convention to convention, but the descriptions provided below capture the general nature of each format.

Poster Sessions

Poster sessions are a relatively new innovation at conventions. Most professional organizations now include posters as

Copyright 1997 David Kelleher.

major parts of their official program offerings. It will help if we begin by describing the physical layout of poster sessions.

A poster session takes place in a large room, sometimes even as large as a hotel ballroom. The room is organized with row after row of poster boards, each about 4 feet by 6 feet in size, often separated from each other by a couple of feet. Each paper to be presented at the session is assigned a poster board. The poster boards are numbered, and the number of a given poster is usually listed in the convention program next to the title of the paper and the name(s) of the author(s), so that you can find a specific poster paper in which you may be interested.

Although the authors of the papers in a poster session are referred to as *presenters*, they do not formally present their material. Instead, they post it. They depict their work, be it a research study or a special treatment technique or innovative training program, visually on a poster board. (See Chapter 6 for information on how to prepare a poster session.) A poster on empirical research might have a brief description of the study, methods, results, and conclusions (in large print) and illustrative tables, charts, and/or figures. A poster on an innovative program might show pictures of the program in action along with a description. Poster presenters are usually asked to have a specified number (e.g., 50 or more) of complete copies of the work available for distribution and to be present at their poster boards to discuss their work with interested people.

So, how does it work? Poster sessions are often (but not always) organized around general topic themes (e.g., assessing productivity in small-scale businesses, working with at-risk youths, gender roles). When this is the case, they all have some area or concern in common, although the connections among individual posters are sometimes rather remote. Thus, if you are interested in a poster session's general theme, you can wander from poster board to poster board, stopping at those of particular interest to collect copies of the papers or discuss the work with the authors. (**Tip:** Authors often run out of papers quickly, as people are apt to pick up anything that is free, even if they are not especially interested in the study. Sometimes, they simply do not want to offend an author by refusing to take a copy. Other presenters may be unprepared and may not have available copies of their papers even if they were required to do so. We do not condone or recommend this unprofessional behavior. Feel free to ask an author to send you a copy of his or her paper.) It is standard for poster presenters to create mailing lists for reprint requests when their supplies of papers have been exhausted. We recommend that you carry a supply of small, adhesive return-address labels; you can affix these to such mailing lists instead of writing out your name and address.

The papers presented at poster sessions at annual conventions, like those given at the paper sessions described below, have usually been chosen through competitive submissions. Individuals submit their work beforehand for a review process—some are accepted and some are not. In reality, however, we suspect that posters are probably easier to get accepted than are spoken papers, because many more can be presented in relatively little time. Presentation of a poster is clearly considered a professional accomplishment, and if you participate in a poster session this should be included on your curriculum vita or résumé.

Convention planners like poster sessions. They note the advantages of the informal setting, in which those attending can interact directly with authors, browse among topics of interest, and pick and choose among posters at which they wish to spend their time. Of course, a major advantage of such sessions is the large number of presentations that can be scheduled into a single hour. We have attended poster sessions with as few as 10 papers and some with as many as 50-100 papers. In the average verbally delivered paper session, four is the absolute maximum that can be presented in a 50-minute hour, so poster sessions greatly increase the number of possible papers and participants.

Attendees at conventions often like poster sessions for the same reasons. Authors, however, are mixed in their reactions. Some prefer the informal setting and the opportunity to chat with others and are just as happy not to have a large and potentially judgmental audience for their formal presentation. Others, however, think paper sessions are more prestigious and would like the opportunity to "perform" in front of an audience. Regardless, the use of poster sessions at conventions is certainly here to stay. Program chairs frequently take submissions for paper sessions and put them into large poster sessions. Sometimes authors are given the option of presenting via posters or not at all.

Other Presentation Formats

There are three basic formats in which papers are *presented,* although not necessarily *read:* paper sessions, panels, and symposia. (See Chapter 6 for information on how to present a paper.) Papers are usually presented in sessions of 50, 90, or 110 minutes. Although there may be slight variations at different professional conferences, each presenter generally has somewhere between 10 and 15 minutes to present his or her material, so all one gets is a brief overview, not a detailed discussion.

Paper sessions. Paper sessions consist of verbal presentations that are grouped together because of some common theme. These presentations were not submitted to the program committee as a package, but as individual papers. The organizers then group them together in the same session because they all address some common topic or concern, such as rational management of irrational people. As a result, the different papers may or may not logically hang together very well, and it is often the case that you may be interested in only one or two of the papers in a given session. (See the discussion of audience etiquette in Chapter 5 for advice on this situation.)

Symposia and panels. Symposia and panels are submitted or invited as "package" presentations. Several people, all doing work on the same topic, agree to present their work in one session. They may or may not be from the same institution or laboratory. As a result, the presentations generally tend to be more related to one another than is often true in paper sessions. A moderator usually makes an overall introduction to the symposium or panel and ties all the presentations together under a common rubric. Symposia frequently have one or more discussants, including the moderator.

There is really little noticeable difference between symposia and panels except that panelists are usually expected to engage in more dialogue among themselves. Sometimes this happens; often it does not.

Formats for Dialogues

Many conventions also feature formats designed to encourage dialogues among people, often among well-established professionals and others interested in their work. These include conversation hours, discussion sessions, roundtables, open forums, and debates.

A *conversation hour* usually features an individual who has attained considerable prominence in a particular area. After initial introductory remarks, the audience is invited to "converse" with that person. Usually, conversation hours are held in relatively intimate small group settings, but this is often not the case when the featured person is a really big name.

Discussion groups are quite similar to conversation hours in that the audience is invited to "discuss" a topic with a key person or persons. Often such a session will feature a panel of speakers, and the discussion may actually be primarily among them. Sometimes the chairs in the meeting room will be arranged in a circular or semicircular pattern as a device to facilitate discussion. **Tip:** You do *not* have to converse at a conversation hour or discuss at a discussion session. If you would rather just sit and listen, your attention will be well appreciated. There will be plenty of people happy to have the floor, and a good listener is always a welcome presence (at conventions and in "real" life).

Roundtables are small group gatherings in which the participants (presenters and "audience") sit at a large, sometimes even a round, table and talk about a topic. Usually, one or more people are designated to present their work briefly, and then the floor is opened for discussion. The presenters have usually submitted the topic for presentation. Sometimes they have been especially invited. At large conventions, this format has the practical advantage that several roundtables, often on topics of interest but expected to have small audiences, can be conducted in the same room. This arrangement makes for an efficient use of time and space.

Open forums in some ways resemble "speak-outs." Usually, one or two people present some thoughts on a specified topic and those in the audience are invited to do the same. There is not much dialogue between people, just an opportunity to share ideas. At some associations' meetings, *debates* are featured between two prominent opponents on some controversial topic in the discipline. For example, is there such a thing as multiple personality disorder, or is Roseanne putting us all on? Or, does painting prisoners' cell walls pink really calm them emotionally, or does it inflame their passions? These sessions can be spontaneous, informative, and fun to listen to for everyone.

Do You Have to Be Invited to Attend an Invited Address?
Prestigious Presentations and Addresses of Honor

Conventions also frequently feature invited addresses by prestigious people in the field. Larger conventions often have many of these, because various subgroups may sponsor several such presentations. *Invited addresses* are just what the name implies: The speaker has been invited to present her or his work or ideas because they are recognized in the field. *Presidential addresses* are presentations by association presidents. (We use the plural because large associations have many sections or divisions, and all of these have presidents, who usually give presidential addresses.) You need not be a member of a particular section or division to attend any invited address. You need only be interested in the topic or in hearing the speaker. Be assured that your presence is most welcome—the larger the audience, the better. Section leaders are most gratified when their audiences include people who are not members.

Award addresses and *award ceremonies* are also major components of conventions. Organizations generally give awards to individuals for outstanding contributions to their fields, and these people may be expected to give addresses, although their talks are often presented in the year following their receipt of the awards. Politicians who head committees promoting bills of interest to certain disciplines may receive special awards from these associations.

Special lecture series are also frequent additions to convention programs. These series are often, but not always, named after famous persons (usually deceased) in the field. It is, of course, an honor to give such a lecture. Sometimes these lectures are centered on particular themes or purposes. The American Psychological Association's G. Stanley Hall Lecture Series, for example, invites lectures designed to inform teachers of introductory psychology classes about the most recent happenings in subfields of psychology, although the talks are usually enlightening for all who are interested in the topic. The Master Lecture Series features "masters" in some subarea, that is, people who have contributed original and valuable work. Whatever the name of the series, these lectures are open to everyone and are almost always worth attending.

Workshops:
Continuing Education Credits and Others

Workshops are a frequently employed format at conventions. Technically, the name *workshop* means that those attending will work—that is, they will actively participate in some way. Many use experiential techniques, for example. You may, however, find yourself sitting in a circle or in a chair in a theater seat arrangement, listening to people present on a topic. Basically, workshops are designed to teach skills or the application of theory.

Workshops are sometimes offered for continuing education credits. Continuing education workshops are more common in fields in which professionals are licensed by the state to practice and are required by that state to continue their professional development or education. Workshops for continuing education are usually monitored for quality by the organization. There is usually a fee for attending a workshop, and registration is required prior to the convention. If space remains at the time a workshop is to begin, additional participants are usually admitted, sometimes at a slightly higher fee. A workshop may last only a few hours, but some continue all day or for several days. The number of continuing education credits an individual receives for attending a workshop is based on how many hours it entails.

Conventions Within Conventions

Certain people or groups may be officially permitted to organize their own themes within a larger convention. These may be referred to as *miniconventions*. For example, the president of the association may be allowed to declare a presidential theme for the convention, such as "Quality of Life Issues for the Elderly." The program committee will then organize a series of presentations on that theme. Some organizations are so large that they have umbrella offices representing different factions of the organization, such as those engaged in education, practice, science, and public interest, and each of these might have a miniconvention within the convention. In other words, each will organize presentations that address its theme for that year and that promote its program. For example, a psychology convention might have a miniconvention on health maintenance organizations, a sociology convention might have one on youth and urban communities, and an anthropology convention might have one on gender, industrialization, and family roles. The larger convention itself may even have an overall theme, such as the role of the association in the next millennium, which is determined by the convention board. Of course, all topics within a discipline usually remain appropriate for submission for presentation at a convention, although those pertaining to the overall theme are generally especially welcomed and promoted.

The content of miniconventions is presented in the same formats we have been discussing. Although references to miniconventions and the like can be intimidating, if you are interested in a particular theme, the convention program book can make it relatively easy for you to locate presentations on that topic by listing them as part of a miniconvention.

Business Meetings and Executive Board Meetings

Most professional associations have sections or divisions, and the members of these meet at annual conventions to conduct their own business and to share with others what they have accomplished during the year. Divisions' executive board meetings include division officers and key committee members of the division or the overall organization. They vote on budgets, determine priorities and policies, and present reports. These meetings can be rather lengthy, and sometimes they are scheduled prior to the official beginning of the convention or toward the end of one of the convention days. If you are interested in the business of a particular division, feel free to go to its meetings. This is also a visible way of getting involved in a division or the overall organization.

Division business meetings are briefer than executive board meetings and provide the officers of the division the opportunity to tell members and anyone else who chooses to attend what the division has done and is planning for the coming year. Attending such meetings is a good way to learn about a division in which you are interested.

Film Programs

Many conventions include screenings of educational and training films as part of the program. The same films may be shown on different days and at different times. Occasionally, these may be major mass-market films that have relevance to the professional interests of the association's members. Often, screenings are followed by directed discussion of the topic from the discipline's perspectives. Attending a screening can be a good evening activity and a pleasant way to spend some time and to meet new people.

Unaffiliated Groups

Sometimes members of groups that are not official parts of the association, but that share common interests, will attend conventions, and may ask for some program time. Usually, this is just for business meetings, because many of their members are also members of the association. It can also provide them with the opportunity to recruit new members. These groups may also sponsor some programs or social hours. Unaffiliated groups might include journal editorial boards, prospective new divisions or interest groups, existing professional associations with overlapping interests, or even "recreational runners" who are organizing morning jogging. The association may provide such groups with courtesy listings in the program, or the groups may post informational fliers around the convention area.

Expanding Program Hours: Hospitality Suites

Some divisions, sections, and other groups reserve suites at convention hotels in which they hold events, such as conversation hours or parties. At these events, informational materials as well as applications for membership in the particular groups involved are almost always available. These *hospitality suites* provide an association's divisions with opportunities to expand their program hours and with settings for social gatherings.

Hospitality suite events are not usually listed in convention programs unless divisions specifically purchase advertising space to promote their activities. Divisions may distribute fliers describing hospitality suite events at the convention site, or division fliers may be included with convention registration materials. Sometimes hospitality suite information is simply posted in convention areas.

Generally, hospitality suite events are relatively informal and provide good opportunities for you to get to know the people active in a given division and to learn more about that division. You do not have to be a member of a division to attend its hospitality suite functions. Divisional members will be delighted if you come to their activities. Sometimes light refreshments or snacks are available in hospitality suites, but the word *hospitality* usually only denotes that you are welcome to visit and chat.

Social Hours

Finally, attending conventions is not all work and papers and intellectual rumination. Association members do socialize. The planners may schedule dances or concerts, and almost always there are cocktail hours (no surprise there). These are frequently referred to as *social hours*. We discuss these social events further in Chapter 7, where we make some suggestions for getting the most out of them.

Summary

Professional associations can be large and complex, and these complexities are reflected in convention programs. Individual convention events, or sessions, take a range of forms, including poster sessions, paper sessions, symposia, panels, debates, conversation hours, and discussion groups. In addition, there may be various invited addresses, lecture series, workshops, and business meetings. Conventions also feature social hours, which give attendees the opportunity to relax, meet people, and socialize. Hospitality suites, sponsored by divisions or sections, further expand opportunities to network and engage in professional dialogue.

We hope that the information provided above will help you to navigate the convention maze more confidently and successfully. Being present at the meeting and assertively participating in it are the best ways to get the most out of your convention experience.

5 | Convention Session Etiquette

Newcomers to professional conventions often are unsure about matters of protocol and polite behavior in sessions. Of course, the usual rules of courtesy and consideration toward others apply at conventions that apply in "real life." Professional association meetings, however, introduce some special circumstances with which new attendees may be unfamiliar. For example, questions arise about such behaviors as arriving late to a session or leaving early, asking questions, describing one's own work, and approaching speakers for more private dialogue. In this chapter we make a few suggestions regarding session etiquette and protocol concerns.

Coming and Going

As we have noted in previous chapters, conventions have many different events going on at the same time, and as a conventioneer you must make decisions about what to attend and what to miss. You cannot do it all. If you are short on time and there is one particular poster that you are interested in, your decision is easy. You can simply march directly to that poster, obtain the information you want, and leave. But what about paper, panel, or symposium sessions? What about conversation hours?

In paper sessions or at symposia or invited addresses (all described in Chapter 4), it is perfectly acceptable to come and go as your interests and schedule dictate. In a paper session, for example, you may be interested in hearing only the third paper of the four listed in the program. In most cases, papers will be presented in the order listed, and you can estimate the length of each and the likely time of the presentation of interest to you. In this way, you can time it so that you arrive shortly before the presentation of interest and, if you like, leave directly after. Similarly, if you are interested in the first paper, you will want to arrive at the session site before the session begins. If the rest of the papers hold little interest for you, you can leave after the first presentation.

When entering or leaving during a session, try to be as minimally disruptive as possible. If you intend to leave before a session is over, consider sitting in the back or on the side, so that you can make a quiet, unobtrusive departure. (This is probably why these sections fill up first, much to the chagrin of the presenters, who often have to address the peripheries of the room.) Although there is no requirement to do so, it usually is polite and less intrusive if you enter or leave a session between presenters rather than during a presentation. Making an ostentatious entrance toward the front of the room, accompanied by comments and interactive conversation, while a speaker is presenting is a matter of discourtesy at the very least. It is appropriate to slip quietly into the room and stand at the back until a presentation is complete, at which time you can proceed to take a seat. Leaving unobtrusively, even during a presentation, is permitted and even recommended, if the topic is insufficiently stimulating or somehow different from what you were expecting. This is more of an issue with lengthy presentations, as most of us can sit through a short, 10-minute talk to avoid disrupting a presentation. Remember, your time is valuable too, and you do not have to suffer or sacrifice unnecessarily. It is assertive to go when you would like to go, for any reason.

Assertiveness becomes aggression, however, when your departure is unnecessarily noisy or noticeable.

One last thought about consideration of others during convention sessions: In recent years there has been a rapid increase in the number of people who rarely emerge from their homes or hotel rooms without their cellular phones close at hand. They have found their way into conventions, and, unfortunately, sometimes into convention sessions as well. It is inconsiderate and inappropriate to hold a telephone conversation, no matter how softly, in a room where someone is presenting. It is hard to believe that anyone would do so, but we have witnessed this. Do not use your cell phone while you are an audience member, and do not be shy about telling someone else to stop doing so. Similarly, if you carry a beeper, keep it on silent or vibration during a session.

Where to Sit During a Session

Try to sit where you can hear the speaker and see any slides or overheads well. Some rooms are quite large, and slides and overheads are often detailed, complex, and printed in tiny type. If you sit near the slide projector, video machine, or wall switches, you may be asked to help focus the projector, adjust a tape's tracking, or perform other technical duties to facilitate the presentation. If you are willing and comfortable doing so (when an audience of dozens to hundreds of people are awaiting your efficient efforts), do not hesitate to sit in those locations. If having to try to correct such glitches will make you uncomfortable (getting the right side up on overheads seems to us always to be the most challenging task), choose a seat sufficiently distant from the equipment. Of course, once committed to assisting, you really should stay until the end of that particular presentation.

As we have mentioned, sitting in the back of the room will allow you to leave unobtrusively if you are unsure about whether you will want to stay for an entire session. Sitting in the back, however, is also usually not very desirable because you may have difficulties in hearing, seeing, and asking questions easily (the speaker will have a microphone, but you probably will not). You will also be distracted by latecomers, early leavers, and water drinkers (many meeting rooms offer ice water, usually placed on tables at the back).

Speakers like large, attentive, enthusiastic audiences. You will represent just one person, unless you travel with a group, as some graduate students prefer to do for familiarity and their own form of social security. The speaker would probably like you to sit in the front of the room and to listen "actively" and with deep appreciation for his or her remarks. We advise you, however, to sit wherever you would like given the considerations we have discussed in this chapter. (**Tip:** One exception to this might be if the presenter is your mentor or someone else you know whom you would like to impress. In that case, front row center may be political wisdom—assuming such politics are not against your principles.)

Finally, for social reasons you may choose to sit next to an interesting-looking person with whom you might decide to apply your conversational skills, as discussed in Chapter 2. Just do not exercise these skills during someone else's presentation.

Questioning the Speaker

Some presenters invite questions at any time, but most prefer to have you hold questions until the end of their presentations. Abide by the speaker's stated wishes. Often a moderator will control the question time by asking that all questions be held until all speakers have completed their presentations. If that is the case, and you do not plan to stay for all the other presentations in that session, your questions properly must go unasked for the time being.

If you have questions that are rather complicated, or if you want advice about your own work, which would be of minimal interest to other audience members, we recommend that you save such questions for personal discussions later or pose them in formal letters to the speaker. It is quite acceptable to write to convention speakers later and without formal introduction. You can note that you heard the presentation and had one or several follow-up questions. You can share your own results briefly or send copies of your own papers on the same topic. If you write such a letter, be sure to include your e-mail address and fax number, if you have them, in your correspondence. Someone else's public talk is not an appropriate forum for describing the details of your own work.

Even if you stay to the end of the session, you may be cheated of the opportunity to ask a question formally. It is not uncommon to run out of time for questions and answers or for only enough time to remain for a couple of questions, in which case you may not be one of the people with a raised hand to catch the moderator's eye. If this happens, feel free to approach the speaker you wanted to address after the session. Keep in mind, however, that everyone will probably have to vacate the room quickly for the next session to begin, and that the speaker may have to race off to another commitment. If that is the case, inquire about contacting the speaker after the convention to discuss the issue more fully.

If you cannot interact with particular speakers during or directly after their presentations, your options are to approach them if and when you encounter them elsewhere at the convention or to write to them at their institutions after the meeting. Audience interest in their work, conveyed via serious and informed questions asked at the convention or in later letters, is usually quite flattering to speakers, even when these individuals are very well known. There's no need for you to be shy about asking your questions. It is assertive and an excellent conversation opener, practically guaranteeing a positive reception. (**Tip:** All professions have their boors. Sometimes a perfectly appropriate question or comment will be met with rude, dismissive behavior. When this happens, it is most likely a statement about the respondent and not you, the initiator. Don't let the possibility of this happening inhibit your initiative, and should it happen, don't let it discourage you from going forward in the next situation.)

Conversation hours and discussion groups offer plenty of opportunities for you to interact with presenters—take advantage of them. Just keep in mind that many people at such events will want the chance to speak and be heard, and monitor yourself to ensure that you do not dominate the session.

Acquiring Papers of Presentations

Sometimes it is impossible for you to attend all of the presentations that you would like to hear or see. Some associations, such as the Speech Communication Association, reproduce and sell copies of all papers scheduled to be presented at their conventions. At these meetings, one need not go to the actual delivery of a paper to obtain the information it contains if one has a schedule conflict (or lunch date). Most conventions do not provide this service, however. In such cases, when you miss the presentation of a paper in which you are interested, it is perfectly appropriate to write to the presenter and request a copy of the paper. There is, of course, no guarantee you will receive one. The presenter may have delivered his or her talk from notes, and may not actually have a complete written version of the presentation. This is particularly likely in the cases of conversation hours and discussion groups, which are not designed for formal presentations. Although it is slightly more expensive and more time-consuming, we think you are probably more likely to get a response from a request for a paper if you send the author a personal letter as opposed to a form-type postcard. It probably also does not hurt to include a stamped, self-addressed return envelope.

As we mentioned in Chapter 4, poster presenters are supposed to have copies of the full reports of their work available. They frequently run out of copies, however, and it is quite appropriate for you to request that such presenters later send you copies of their reports. (**Tip:** Carrying a supply of adhesive return-address labels is a convenient and practical means of providing your mailing information on lists of requests for copies. It is particularly wise if your handwriting is difficult to decipher.)

Stephen J. Danyko and Dean McKay, two behavioral psychologists, investigated the reprint request process at the 1993 national convention of the Association for the Advancement of Behavior Therapy. They requested reprints from 158 poster presenters at the meeting who had already run out of copies of their papers and who then gathered lists of requests for copies. Danyko and McKay wanted to study whether the requester's giving a home versus an institutional return address, and whether or not the requester held a Ph.D., made any difference in requesters' receipt of requested papers.

Their findings, published in the October 1994 issue of *the Behavior Therapist*, revealed that the nature of the requester's address and his or her degree status made no difference in whether or not the requester received requested papers. Papers were sent, regardless of the condition, only about half the time. Thus requesting a copy of a paper, which is normal and appropriate to do, is hardly a guarantee that one will actually be sent. The relatively low compliance with requests for papers found by Danyko and McKay is especially surprising because the presenters had explicitly offered to send the copies, it is ethical professional behavior to fulfill those requests, and the meeting was a gathering of behaviorists, who investigate compliance behavior as part of their discipline.

How can you increase the compliance rates of presenters from whom you request copies of their work? In contrast to Danyko and McKay, we have not engaged in formal research on this general topic. However, we recommend that you establish a personal connection with each presenter as you make the request. Engage the presenter in a bit of conversation about his or her work, and you will become salient to him or her. When you write to the presenter, you can mention your conversation at the meeting and your interest in his or her work. Thus your letter will accrue more personal meaning. Of course, this friendly follow-up letter would be sent only after your having left your address on the presenter's master list did not produce a response within a reasonable time (e.g., 3 to 4 weeks). As suggested above, you may also want to consider enclosing a stamped, self-addressed return envelope.

Convention Attire

Most meetings have no special dress code. A relevant factor is the location of the meeting. The style of dress, for both presenters and audiences, tends to be much more informal in Miami and Honolulu than in Boston or New York City, for example. Other than in tropical settings, shorts, T-shirts, halter tops, and thongs are usually out of order. Different groups observe different dress codes. For example, conventions of the Academy of Management and meetings of political scientists tend to be more formal than those of psychologists, which are more formal than those of sociologists and anthropologists. If you are unsure whether your group tends toward more formal or informal convention dress, ask someone who has attended that particular convention. Be comfortable, but give careful consideration to dressing professionally, particularly if you may want to impress a potential future employer or collaborator.

Ordinarily, if you are making a presentation, you will dress more formally than those coming to hear you. Although this will vary at different conventions, depending on the group meeting, usually male presenters will wear jackets and ties and female presenters will wear suits or other "professional" office attire.

Recording Sessions

Many meetings have policies regarding the recording of sessions, and any tape-recording may require permission in advance. Check with convention organizers to find out the policy before you record a session (this information may also be in the convention program). Assuming you are allowed to record sessions, always also ask permission from the speakers first. Additionally, you will probably be allowed to record only the presentation and not the discussion that follows. Obey these rules. Aside from the need to be considerate and to respect the privacy rights of the people in the audience who may ask questions or make comments, there may be copyright considerations involved.

Obviously, most speakers will object to your taping if you are planning to sell the tapes. Unless you have a special arrangement with the convention organizers, any recordings you make are for your own use and cannot be distributed. Under these circumstances, most speakers will give permission. If any will not, you will have to rely only on your note-taking skills in those sessions. (**Tip:** If you are recording for your own use, you will most likely have to bring your own recorder and tape. Because you will probably be recording from your seat, you will need a sensitive machine and should take care to choose your seat accordingly. Special arrangements for recording sessions can usually be made for those who are hearing impaired.)

At many conventions, professional recording services are now making audio- and/or videotapes of some, if not all, of the presentations. Of course, these recordings are then offered for sale by the companies who made them. If you want such a professional-quality recording of any particular session, ordering on the premises sometimes will get you a discount price.

Summary

Feel free to enter and leave sessions that are in progress, only do so quietly and unobtrusively. If you stay until the end of a session and time permits, you can ask questions, but you are also encouraged to approach speakers after their sessions or to contact them after the convention to pursue interaction about your work and theirs. Requesting copies of presenters' papers is also appropriate, although you may or may not receive every paper you request. When choosing a seat at a session, balance the need to hear and see against the possibility that you may want to leave early. Although it is often desirable to take home a recording of an interesting speaker, you must follow convention rules and obtain presenters' permission before you record any sessions. Finally, like it or not, many people will make judgments about you based on how you are dressed. Consider your attire in the context of the larger group norm and your goals for the convention.

6 | Surviving Your Own Professional Presentation

Presenting your work and ideas to your professional colleagues, many of whom may be distinguished and very senior to yourself, can be intimidating if you are new to conventions. You might develop serious doubts about your professional knowledge or your ability to speak coherently under pressure. Most of these anxieties are normal and will dissipate after you have had a few experiences presenting at meetings, as long as you don't let them frighten you away forever at the beginning. The treatment for "normal" presentation anxiety is simple: practice and preparation.

To be sure, some people suffer from more serious and debilitating public speaking phobias. There are effective professional treatments available for them, such as systematic desensitization therapy. Our concern here, however, is more with the stomach butterflies and other very common feelings of nervousness most people feel when they try on a task at which they have little or no experience in a public setting.

Beyond the content of your work, *it is all in the presentation*. Often high-quality, original, and contributory work is undervalued because of a boring or disorganized presentation. Similarly, a dynamic and engaging presentation can leave many with the opinion that a rather ordinary piece of work is the product of genius. It takes a true convention diehard (or perhaps a favored student) to attend closely enough to the verbal ramblings of a prolix speaker in order to sift out the talk's important core. On the other hand, we all like to be engaged and entertained by what we hear or read and want to come away from any presentation feeling that we have followed the flow and learned something new.

There Is No
Substitute for Preparation

The key—indeed, the essential ingredient—to a successful poster or oral presentation is *preparation*. There is no substitute for it and no way around it. Rare is the individual who can deliver a professional talk effectively without preparation. Don't be fooled by the casual speaker who presents without notes. If the presentation goes well, you can assume careful preparation preceded it. Of course, someone who has given a particular talk many times before may not prepare diligently for each presentation, but delivering a talk many times is itself a lot of preparation. Furthermore, even in such a situation there is the risk that the speaker will take the success of the talk for granted and, as a result, the presentation may be sloppy.

Many presenters will tell you that they have not prepared, but you shouldn't necessarily always believe them. You will have a better idea if this is true in particular cases after you have heard the presentations. It is not uncommon for people to run around a convention saying they haven't finished writing their presentations yet, or that they are just going to speak off-the-cuff. When these remarks are true, it is unfortunate. Often, however, people tend to make such comments even when they have given considerable time and thought to their presentations.

There are three common reasons some people may profess lack of preparation. First, they may be perfectionists, and no matter how much preparation they do, they believe it is never enough. Such people experience considerable anxiety until their presentations are over. Others are afraid that their presentations will not go well and they want a handy excuse, one that will be more believable if provided before the fact. Finally, there are those who think that claiming to be unprepared is "cool" and a measure of their self-confidence. However you decide to represent your own state of readiness, the reality should be that you have carefully and thoroughly prepared for your presentation. We suggest below some techniques you can use to do this.

Preparation takes time. Unless you were called in at the last minute to fill in for someone who suddenly could not attend the convention (a rare occurrence), you will have plenty of time to prepare. There is generally a quite generous time gap between notification that your paper has been accepted, or an invitation to present your work, and the first day of the convention. (**Tip:** Sometimes people submit presentation proposals for work that is in progress. We suggest you be cautious about doing this unless you are certain that the work will be completed, with sufficient time to write it up, before the convention.) The amount of time between confirmation that your paper has been accepted and the day it is to be delivered may tend to encourage procrastination. If you know you have a tendency to procrastinate, fight the urge! Before you realize it, you will awaken one morning with the Big Day looming in front of you.

Although some very exceptional people can pull it off, for most of us, papers prepared at the last minute are never as good as those to which we have devoted significant time and effort. Poster session presentations are likely to be sloppy, less attractive than they could be, and difficult to follow. Oral presentations tend to be poorly timed (notice presenters who start skipping pages toward the end of their talks), less coherent, and less engaging than they should be. Additionally, it is a real drag to be still working on your paper after you arrive at the convention, because this leaves you less time to enjoy the convention and attend to your other goals. It also contributes to a pervasive anxiety that can cast an unpleasant shadow over your whole convention experience. Finally, if you are still working on your first draft when the convention begins, you won't have the opportunity to put it aside in order to get some distance from it before you return to it for final editing and rehearsal.

Remember, one way or another, when your time comes to present, you have made a commitment to be there. This is not a publication deadline that you can get extended, or a course where you can take an "incomplete." Excuses won't work. If, for some unavoidable emergency reason, you cannot attend the convention, you are expected to send (fax, if necessary) a copy of your paper for someone else to read. On the other hand, if you are prepared, the rest is a breeze, and you can relax and go about your convention business with ease.

Preparing a Poster
That Attracts and Informs

We have described poster sessions in Chapter 4. To reiterate, each poster in a session usually is presented on a board, about 4 feet by 6 feet, supported on an easel. Your responsibility is to depict your presentation visually on the board. Tacks may or may not be provided for you to pin your presentation materials onto the board, so if you don't know for sure that tacks will be available, bring some along. Your goal is to allow a person who reads your board to learn, without struggle, what was done, how it was done, and what the outcome was.

In past poster sessions, we have observed presentations in which authors have simply tacked complete typed papers on their boards. An interested individual has to stand about a foot from the board to read such a paper. This blocks others from seeing the work and is hard on the eyes; further, such a display is boring and discourages interest. This is not the intent of poster sessions, and we strongly urge you not to present at such sessions in this way (we would forbid such presentations if we were in a position to do so).

A poster session presentation should be attractive and easy to read. It should contain only key points and should include both written and graphic or tabular material. All of this should be enlarged so that it is clear to a person of average eyesight standing 6 feet in front of the poster. For example, a poster presentation of empirical research might be set up as follows. Along the top of the poster board, in large print, is the name of the study. The authors' names and their affiliations may come below this in smaller print. Going from left to right below that, there might then be a brief summary of the goals of the study, with a few sentences laying out the rationale. Next should be the methodology, in outline form. If the study tested a theoretical model, this might be depicted in graph or chart format, rather than in written text (although a brief written description might be required in the goals section of the poster). Results can be presented most easily and parsimoniously in tables or graphs (with important ones highlighted), although it is usually helpful if key findings are noted in written outline form. The final components should be a very brief summary and the study conclusions.

The same principles apply if the poster presentation describes not research but a project or program. The poster can simply be modified accordingly. For example, pictures might be included of the program in action, or charts or sketches depicting key principles and relationships.

When creating a poster presentation, it is useful to use color and varying print sizes, keeping some kind of system in mind. For example, these techniques can be used to highlight important points, to section off different parts of the presentation, or to indicate some form of order. This will also contribute to the attractiveness of the poster and, as a result, the attention it will receive.

We encourage you to tack up your poster and review it as a run-through before you arrive at the convention, and to do so while you still have sufficient time for final modifications. This is part of preparation. It will give you an opportunity to see if all the parts fit together easily and to determine whether you have settled on the best placement for each item. You do not want to start making these decisions and moving things around when you arrive at your poster session. This preparation will also allow you to determine if the material is easily comprehensible and the presentation sequence the best. It is at this time that you can judge, "What is missing? What is unnecessary? What would make this more attractive?"

Finally, many convention planners require that you also have copies of the written paper on which your poster is based to distribute to interested conventioneers. This can be in summary form, but it should have all the relevant and important points included. Also, don't be surprised if you run out of papers. People readily pick up available papers, sometimes simply because they are free. Other times, people take them because they are concerned they will insult you if they do not. Therefore, be prepared to take names and addresses so you can later mail copies to those who request them. (**Tip:** One idea that will make life easier for you when you return home is to take mailing labels to the poster session and have people who want copies of your paper write their names and addresses on them. Then you can simply put copies into envelopes and attach mailing labels, without having to rewrite addresses. An additional benefit is that you won't have to try to decipher people's handwriting.

Presenting a Paper
Without Losing Your Audience

Before you even begin preparing for an oral paper presentation, find out how much time you will have to present. This is usually easy to figure out. For example, if your paper session is placed in a 50-minute slot and there are four presenters (discussants count as presenters), then you will probably have 10 minutes maximum for your presentation. Chairs of sessions generally try to leave a few minutes for questions, and there are sometimes delays (e.g., clearing out people from the previous session, which reflects the inconsideration of these people) as well as a few minutes of introduction from the session chair. In addition, you can always call the chair of your session months in advance and ask how much time you will have. For symposia or panels, for example, the chair may want to have shorter presentations to allow time for panel dialogue. Check to be sure.

Unless you are an invited speaker, or for some special reason have been granted considerable time, you will probably have to condense your talk into a very limited amount of time—undoubtedly a lot less than you would like (or even need) to present your work fully. Still, you will have no choice, so here are some tips on how to do this and still remain interesting and informative in your talk.

First, we strongly urge you to prepare a talk that you can complete well within the allotted time. Focus on the most important points you want to make. Many people barely get through their introductory comments and background information before their time is up. There is nothing more frustrating than having only one minute left to summarize what you did and what you found. It is not uncommon to hear a presenter start rapidly reading a paper and skipping pages in order to finish on time. Running over your time allocation is unacceptable. If you run long, you shorten the time available for either the last presenter or the session's question period. Or, worse yet, the whole session will run late and cut into the one that follows. A session chair who is doing his or her job will not allow you to take more than your allotted time. A good chair will keep you aware of your time restraints by slipping written notes in front of you—"3 minutes," "1 minute," "Time is up."

When putting together your talk, concentrate on the central points that are the core contribution of your work, that is, the information that makes your paper worth presenting to others. Focus on what is original and interesting about your work. This is not the time to get carried away with literature reviews or to describe methodology in excruciating detail. When making an oral presentation, just mention the one or two studies, or theories, that were critical to the genesis of your work. It may *all* appear important to you, but you need to determine what are the most important points to convey.

It is essential that you rehearse your talk, that you do so aloud, and that you do so many times. Rehearse with slides or overheads if they are to be part of your presentation. (**Tip:** If possible, rehearse in front of someone or several people. This will better prepare you for the real thing, and your rehearsal audience can give you feedback.)

Rehearse with a tape recorder, so you can play the presentation back and hear how you sound. Speakers new to presenting at conventions often try to get by without using a microphone because of their unfamiliarity with such equipment. When a session has more than 10 people in the audience, it is almost always best for you to use a microphone, so your voice will reach everyone easily and clearly. No one will have to strain to listen, and you will not have to strain to speak loudly.

It would be most helpful if you rehearse with the type of recorder that requires speaking into a microphone, as you will be doing this during your presentation. It can be rather unsettling to speakers to hear their own voices (and even their breathing) electronically amplified. Also, some consonants (e.g., *p* and *d*) can be quite explosive when spoken into a microphone. Practicing with a tape recorder that requires you to use a microphone will provide you the opportunity to hear which words require modified enunciation.

If you plan to use slides, videotape, or overheads as part of your presentation, it is crucial that you practice with the equipment so you will be able to operate it smoothly. Visual aids can greatly enhance a presentation, but only if they can be integrated smoothly with your talk. It is always disconcerting to everyone when slides flash out of order or upside down, or

Table 6.1 Advice on Delivering Presentations

When you are presenting in a poster session

Construct posters to include the following:

1. the title of your presentation,
2. the name(s) of the author(s) and their affiliations, and
3. a description of the work that highlights the major elements covered.

Have handouts available. Ideally, these should be in the form of a research or project/program report.

Exploit the opportunities provided by this visual mode of presentation:

1. Pictures, tables, and figures are amenable to poster display.
2. Use color in your visuals.
3. Make sure that your lettering is neat and large enough to be read from a distance.
4. Consider using a flowchart or some other method of providing a guide to inspection of your display.
5. Do not overwhelm with excessive amounts of information.

During the poster session, be stationed by your poster.

When you are presenting a paper

Recognize the constraints imposed on your presentation:

1. the short time limit for your presentation;
2. the limits on attention and comprehension of your audience, who are listening to many presentations each day, some of which are outside their area of expertise; and
3. the context of the session, in which people may enter and leave at any time, causing distractions and a less-than-ideal listening-learning situation.

when other common presentation glitches arise. Your own discomfort at these events will create sympathetic anxieties in your

Table 6.1 *Continued*

When preparing your talk, do the following:

1. Decide on a limited number of significant ideas that you want your audience to code, comprehend, and remember.
2. Minimize details while highlighting the main ideas you want to transmit.
3. State clearly in simple, jargon-free terms what the point of the research or project is, what you discovered, and what you think it means.
4. Employ some redundancy—that is, repeat important ideas—to enhance comprehension and recall.
5. Write out your presentation as a minilecture, starting with an outline that you expand into a narrative.
6. Practice delivering your talk aloud in order to learn it, make its length fit the time allocated, and hear how it sounds.
7. Get feedback both from tape-recorded replay of your delivery and from colleagues who listen to it.
8. Try not to read your paper. Speak your ideas directly to your audience, referring, if necessary, to an outline of key points and transitions.
9. Try to speak loudly enough, clearly enough, and with sufficient enthusiasm to hold the attention of your audience despite distractions.
10. State your final conclusions and end on time.

Have available for distribution copies of a version of your paper and/or a sign-up sheet on which interested people can request the paper.

SOURCE: Adapted from a convention handout distributed at an annual meeting of the Western Psychological Association.

listeners, who will begin to focus on your distress and not on the content of your presentation. We also recommend that you use a pocket-sized laser light pointer to direct audience attention to key areas on your slides or other projected materials. This device makes it easier for the audience to follow your presentation, and your practiced professional delivery will surely impress.

Even when we think we are rehearsing silently at the same rate we will speak, we rarely are. Silent rehearsals take less time than spoken ones, and if you rely on them you are likely to find that your oral presentation takes a lot longer than you anticipated. Rehearse aloud until your presentation goes smoothly and is well within the time limit. Include in your rehearsals any asides you may be tempted to add.

Seasoned teachers often adopt a didactic presentation style, in which they essentially teach the material as if they were lecturing to a graduate class. This approach can be interesting and engaging. It is perfectly acceptable, however, simply to report your work, particularly if you are uncomfortable or inexperienced at public speaking (or just prefer this style of presentation). Either way, the effectiveness of your presentation will depend on practice.

Do you read your paper or do you "talk" it? A lot of this depends on how dramatic a reader you are and how dynamic a speaker you are. Nonetheless, "talked" papers are usually more engaging, and we encourage you to strive for this delivery. Papers that are read can be (but are not necessarily) boring. If you decide to read your paper, give special attention to sentence structure, pauses, and emphasis on key words. Writing a paper for oral presentation is very different from writing something that others will read for themselves.

"Talking" a paper does require more work of you, in order to make sure you cover what you want to and in the time allotted. If you choose this route, we recommend working from a detailed outline. A workable compromise is to combine the two delivery styles. With your written paper in front of you with the key points highlighted (i.e., marked with a highlighting pen), you are free to glance down in order to stay on track and not miss something important while you fill the rest in more spontaneously. Whether you read or talk your presentation, or some combination of the two, rehearsing is the key to success.

If you are shortening a longer paper for your presentation, we strongly suggest you retype the original so that it contains only the material you intend to present. Otherwise, you will end up flipping through, and being distracted by, material you had intended to delete. One final suggestion: A few humorous remarks, interesting anecdotes, or interesting asides are usually received with appreciation by audiences. Humor is well-known to create a positive learning environment.

The Roles of Session Chair and Discussant

Chairing a session is an easy way to get your name in the convention program while doing little work. Nonetheless, the position of chair has responsibilities, and a good chair can make a difference in the total quality of a session. A conscientious chair will inform the people presenting long before the convention about the amount of time they have to present and assure them that she or he will require that they abide by time limits. An effective chair gets the session started on time. (**Tip:** If you are a session chair, arrive at your site as the preceding session is ending, so that you can usher out the people who may be lingering and speaking to the presenters from that session.)

The chair begins the session with a few sentences on what the session is about and then introduces the speakers. Sometimes the speakers are all introduced at the beginning, but more commonly each is introduced as he or she is called upon to present. This may require that each speaker go up to a podium, or all may speak from a dais, depending upon the format of the session. An effective chair keeps presenters within time limits by unobtrusively passing them time warning notes. If a speaker continues past his or her allotted time, the chair may find it helpful to nudge a little, perhaps by standing up. (**Tip:** If you are chair of a session, seat yourself next to the podium, so you can slip notes to speakers unobtrusively.) The chair is also responsible for moderating the question-and-answer time and for seeing to it that the session ends on time (e.g., "We will take one more question and then we will have to stop. You can continue your discussion outside the room if you like.").

Being a discussant is more demanding than being a session chair. The role of discussant is usually filled by a recognized expert in the field. Technically, a discussant should receive the presenters' papers before the convention, with sufficient time to prepare a discussion based on them. This usually entails commenting about each paper and/or the general theme that ties them all together, as well as adding some original thoughts on the topic.

Unfortunately, many presenters do not finish their papers early enough to get them to their sessions' discussants in advance. If you are a discussant, feel free to nag presenters for their papers. If, however, you fail in this attempt, you will have to combine two approaches—one is preparation; the other is winging it.

You may notice that discussants often sit on the dais taking notes as the presenters give their papers; they are preparing the discussion. That is, they are noting the key points the speakers are making for the purpose of later discussing the papers. Discussants try to draw the key points of a session together and comment on each and/or on the topic as a whole. We strongly suggest, however, that if you are a discussant, even when you have not received presenters' papers beforehand, you prepare in advance. Have a general outline of your thoughts on the topic and a few major points you would like to make about it. Fit appropriate references to the papers into this outline wherever possible. If the presenters feel you have given too little time to their talks, perhaps they will learn a lesson that will benefit the next discussant who must address their work.

Summary

Presenting at a professional conference is work. It is part of your work as a professional and it comes with professional credit. It is work, but it is not difficult—it simply requires thought and preparation. The more you do it, the easier it gets. It is almost always gratifying, and it can be exhilarating.

We urge you to submit proposals to your professional conferences and to present papers whenever you are given the opportunity. We are hopeful that the points we have made in this chapter will help you to enjoy the experience and to do it well.

7 | Meeting Your Social Needs

At first blush, it might seem immature to be concerned about meeting one's social needs at a professional conference. It certainly is an almost taboo topic, rarely talked about. We might discuss the professional aspects of conventions with our mentors, but how often do we feel sufficiently comfortable to utter such words as "How do I find companionship for dinner?" The very thought of spending five nights eating alone in a restaurant can be distressing, but because our motives for attending conventions are ostensibly professional ones, voicing such concerns seems childish and dependent. They are, however, very legitimate concerns, and addressing them is central to our getting the most out of a convention. We humans, after all, are social animals.

Conventions can be lonely, and the larger they are, the lonelier they can be. For example, the American Psychological Association's annual convention typically draws more than 15,000 registrants to one of the few North American cities large enough to accommodate such a meeting. There are few experiences as distressing as feeling alone in a crowd, but it is precisely in a crowd that it can be most difficult to connect socially. Many people who attend conventions cope with these feelings of loneliness by keeping as busy as possible, running from one event to the next, leaving little time for conversation and assuring exhaustion so that an early sleep becomes a welcome end to the day. Rarely do these attendees think back on conventions fondly, and rarely do they look forward to the next one. Others confront the possibility of loneliness by going to conventions with someone else. This strategy can be advisable, but it is not always possible. Additionally, it, too, can create problems. Your traveling companion may have social interests and goals very different from yours. Or you could become so wedded to a companion that you block opportunities to meet other convention attendees who may share similar interests. Ultimately, social needs at a convention overlap with professional needs, for social activities are valuable opportunities for you to develop a professional network and establish professional friendships.

Finding Informal
Social Support Groups

Most large associations have subgroups that represent special concerns, and these can be a rich resource from which to develop informal social support groups. For example, student organizations are a welcome body for students. They are sensitive to student concerns and their realities at conventions. Women's issues groups and ethnic concern groups generally hold formal and informal meetings and share common experiences and concerns within the profession. You can check the program, bulletin boards, and postings of related activities to find these groups and take advantage of them and the settings they provide. This will very much enrich your convention experience and expand your professional network.

Convention planners are well aware of the importance of providing for people's social needs. They want people to laugh and have fun and meet in informal, relaxed settings. They want people to enjoy the convention. They are cognizant of the fact that the more successful they are in achieving this, the more likely the convention will be considered a success and people will return to the next meeting and encourage others to do the same. Consequently, convention planners schedule dances, concerts, and/or local sightseeing trips. There are almost always cocktail hours or receptions, but not all of them will be mentioned in the formal convention program.

Social Hours, Receptions, and Dances

"Social hours" are cocktail hours. They may be sponsored by the association's convention planners or, in larger associations, by individual groups or divisions. Several may take place at the same time, sometimes in adjacent rooms.

Social hours almost always have a cash bar (no discounts found here). The "richer" groups may serve something to munch on, but when they do, there is rarely enough for everyone attending, so if you are hungry, get there early. Receptions are similar to social hours, but they are more likely to serve something edible (which may be one of the reasons they are fewer than social hours). Receptions may also feature brief greetings, announcements, and short testimonials to honored guests or members.

You do not have to be a member of a group to attend its social hour. On the contrary, the more the merrier. You can buy a drink at one gathering and saunter into another with your drink in hand (as long as this does not entail walking outdoors in a state that forbids alcohol consumption on the street). Social hours are good places to catch up with people, meet new people, and discuss your own and others' work in an informal setting. (**Tip:** Do not get too intense at a social hour; everyone is trying to unwind.) Social hours are also excellent places to look for dinner companionship.

Although you are welcome at all social hours, it might be advantageous to attend those sponsored by groups representing concerns of interest to you. There you are likely to find people with similar interests or perspectives (e.g., research methodologies, gender issues, ethnic concerns) and to cross paths with distinguished scholars and researchers in the area. The informal setting will also give you a chance to learn more about the subgroup and to decide whether you want to become a member.

Some conventions have dances. There is often an admission charge (which is usually listed in the convention program) for a dance and, once more, usually a cash bar. If it is a dinner dance, that feature will be stated in the program and admission priced accordingly. Dress codes will vary for dances, but if there is no hint about dress in the program and you cannot find someone to ask who has attended a dance at that convention in the past, play it safe and lean toward party dress-up.

Because of the music, which usually makes even light discourse difficult without yelling, and the fact that people will seat themselves at tables, it is more difficult at dances than at social hours to converse with people you have just met. On the other hand, people at dances are usually in a party mood, which encourages friendliness (as does the availability of alcohol). Regardless, dances provide great opportunities for you to dance and have fun. And, in present times, at many conventions' dances (e.g., those held by historians, psychologists, sociologists, and literary groups) there are few gender or sexual orientation dance etiquette behavioral restrictions. It matters not who asks whom to dance or who dances with whom. (**Tip:** This may not apply to conventions of bankers, politicians, stock brokers, salespeople, or fundamentalist ministers, so use your judgment within the context of the group and your goals.) Just get on the dance floor and have a good time. Many a friendship has begun at a convention dance, but, eventual friendship or no friendship, dancing itself is fun and burns off those calories from dinner!

Finding Dinner and Touring Companions

The two activities that people seem most interested in finding companionship for at conventions are "seeing the town" and dining. (An obvious additional activity, romance, is discussed below.) Conventions are usually held in interesting cities, and it can enhance the convention experience to set aside a morning or afternoon (or more) to see some of the highlights of the area. If you do not want to take time away from the convention, consider arriving a day early or staying a day later. Taking an organized tour, put together by a local travel agency, is one way to go. It is efficient, particularly if you do not have much time, and the details of travel are someone else's responsibility. Your travel companions will probably consist of others from your convention as well as other visitors to the city. Local hotels can connect you with such tours. You might also take tours sponsored by the convention planners. These will probably emphasize sights of particular interest to association members, and the people on the tour with you will be other convention attendees and their families and friends.

Some people do not like organized tours. The selection of places visited on a tour may not reflect their interests, or they may not enjoy the rigidity of time and place or traveling with strangers. Many prefer the adventure of negotiating a city by themselves, experimenting with an unfamiliar transit system, and exploring unique sights and neighborhoods at their own pace.

It is not uncommon for people to be uncomfortable when eating out alone. Having breakfast and lunch alone in a local coffee shop seems to be easier than eating dinner alone, if not easy. However, dinner in a local restaurant in a different section of the city, or even in one of the finer restaurants in a convention hotel, without companionship, is often unappealing. As a result, many convention attendees just grab a quick bite in the same coffee shop or deli they have been frequenting for breakfast and lunch. Others who can afford it may take the room service route and spend quiet evenings in their rooms (and may prefer to do so). This is great when it is what you want to do (and it may well be after a tiring day), but it is unfortunate when you would really prefer to be out and about. After a busy day at the convention, it can be enjoyable and rewarding to have companionship for leisurely eating, talking, and sharing of convention experiences. What is more, dining with a newly met colleague is one way of firmly establishing an acquaintance relationship that will become part of an expanding professional network. As such, dining with another can be both pleasure and "business."

Anytime you have an opportunity to start up a conversation with another person attending the convention is a good time to find dinner companionship. Lining up company for touring usually requires getting to know someone a little better (perhaps if you dine together and find that you are compatible), because the time spent together is usually longer and some negotiating is generally involved. Social hours and receptions are good places to find someone to join you for dinner. They are conducive to chatting, as people typically just mill around. It is usually easier to engage another solo person in dialogue than to break into a larger group if you know no one in that group. If you do succeed in partaking in a group dialogue, it is common and courteous for the whole group to head out to dinner and invite you along. (**Tip:** Don't wait to be invited. It is easy to say, "Do you have dinner plans tonight?" Also, don't be insulted if the person you address politely declines with a rather transparent excuse. People frequently use conventions to catch up with old friends or talk professional shop with a specific agenda that would be inhibited by the presence of others. Their dinner plans could have been made weeks earlier. Just keep talking, being friendly, and ask someone else.)

Other places are also conducive to finding eating and touring companions. The gatherings at divisional or special interest group hospitality suites, mentioned in Chapter 4, are designed to be informal. In suites that remain open and active, people often hang around and chat. Even the lobby or bar of a convention hotel can be a meeting place, but this will work only if you appear open and socially receptive. If your nose is buried in the convention program, you are less approachable.

Our main point is, anyplace can be a meeting place. You just have to be available to meet someone. And it is not always necessary or wise to think strictly in terms of dinner. Dinner can be too much of a commitment for someone with whom you have had merely a few words. If you find yourself engaged in discussion about an interesting paper you heard with someone else who was present, suggesting that you continue the discussion over a cup of coffee or a drink might result in a nice break in pace.

As you should well know, one-on-one dining is a different experience from dining with a group. The differences are obvious, but you should consider them in accepting or offering a dinner engagement. Dining with one other person, as opposed to several, can be more intimate, which may or may not be comfortable or desirable for you. After all, the person may be, for all practical purposes, almost a stranger (or someone you don't completely trust). The experience can also end up simply being boring, with escape delayed until after coffee and dessert. It is, on the other hand, an opportunity to get to know someone better and perhaps to make a professional, if not personal, friend. Group dining is less intimate and is often higher energy and more dynamic. (**Tip:** The decision about "check splitting" versus separate checks when dining in groups can be problematic for many people. Many people do not want, or cannot afford, to "subsidize" more exuberant appetites, but it can be awkward to ask for a separate check when others agree that splitting the total is easier. If this is a concern for you, try to get clarification beforehand. This advice also applies to the prices at the chosen restaurant.)

Sometimes you may not find dining or touring companionship, or you genuinely may not want it some evenings. After a full day surrounded by people, dining and touring alone also can be very enjoyable, and we encourage it (just check out the locations for safety). You can do what you want on your own schedule and be spared the need to make small talk or to pretend interest. Take some light reading along if you fear filling the time between soup and entrée.

Romance and Convention Affairs

It does happen! Some people find romance at conventions, and some people have "convention affairs." Such affairs may be limited to one convention or can become an annual convention event ("same time next year"). We have no idea of how frequently this happens. We know of no research that would shed light on this behavior, but we would like to share a few observations.

Conventions can be ripe for romance, although we suspect simple, uncomplicated affairs or flings are more the norm. People are away from home (a wise old analyst friend used to say, "Superegos don't travel"), and those attending the convention share a common discipline. Thus, they are likely to meet people whose interests overlap their own. The attendance of interesting people from across the nation, sometimes the world, makes it easier to engage in somewhat superficial relationships designed simply for fun and pleasure, free from long-term obligations and expectations. The possibility of feeling lonely contributes to receptiveness for intimacy.

Some people actively seek convention affairs with no strings attached. Others are mildly receptive should desirable opportunities present themselves. And still others are unprepared and caught somewhat off guard. Keep in mind that not all, or perhaps even most, of the players are single. Indeed, many are married or have partners, and the convention becomes their playground for a potential annual fling. This fact of life may or may not be objectionable to you; all we are saying is, be aware.

If you are in an exclusive relationship but are pursuing, or just finding yourself seriously considering, a convention affair, we strongly urge you to mention your ongoing relationship to your prospective convention partner. This is not simply an issue of fairness—that is, giving the other person the right to decide with information he or she may consider relevant (which is reason enough)—it is also self-protective. Keep in mind that whereas one person's perspective on this liaison may be that it is a fling, with no strings attached and no future considered, the other person may have a range of very different expectations. This issue is no different from the courting games that are played at home, but there may be elements at a convention that people sometimes think give them license they do not enjoy at home. For example, people at a convention may experience a degree of anonymity that they don't have in their hometowns, and others might actually flaunt their freedom in front of colleagues. Be clear about what you want and go into it with a high level of reality checking. Remember, you may well see this person again, in another setting (particularly if you come from the same institution), and the behaviors that seemed acceptable at the convention may later be a cause of discomfort and embarrassment.

Nonetheless, many a "true romance" has begun at conventions, and many have developed into long and enduring friendships. These days, particularly among academicians, long-distance relationships are not rare.

Finally, we feel compelled to remind you to practice safe sex should the opportunity present itself. We are all aware that AIDS is not limited to a particular social class, ethnicity, gender, or profession. Nonetheless, there is a strong tendency to believe that people like ourselves, or nice, clean-cut, professional, and achieving people, are safe from sexually transmitted diseases. You know you should know better, so *know better*. Whether you are female or male, be prepared.

Sexual Harassment and Exploitation

It is unfortunate, but not surprising, that conventions are not without their incidents of sexual harassment and potential sexual exploitation. Like work and learning settings, a convention has a hierarchy of power and status, and where this exists, the potential for its abuse is present. At a convention, however, incidents of the abuse of power take on a somewhat different tone from that found in other settings. For one thing, the atmosphere at a convention tends to be rather congenial and informal, resulting in a blurring of roles. There is often a pretense of equality among colleagues and a professed attitude that the rules (away from home) may be somewhat different. In this domain, they really are not.

Without getting into definitions of sexual harassment and debates about what constitutes it (for more information about this, see Michele Paludi's informative edited book *Sexual Harassment on College Campuses: Abusing the Ivory Power,* SUNY Press, 1996), we would like to outline some of the dynamics that can, and have, occurred at conventions.

Students have reported, at best, distress and disappointment and, at worst, actual conflict and negative consequences, when a trusted professor or mentor has shifted the rules of the game at a convention. There are many forms this can take. The professor may have encouraged the student to attend the convention, perhaps coauthored a paper with the student, taken the opportunity to show the student the ropes, made introductions to colleagues, and so forth. Although this is good mentoring and we encourage it, it has a whole different meaning when the intent is to demonstrate power and the potential to advance the student's career for the purpose of establishing a sexual relationship. Even if the student willingly consents to such a relationship, it seems to us to be an abuse of power, and, as recent legislation indicates, it could be grounds for sexual harassment charges. Whether or not the student engages in sexual relations with the professor, back on campus or in the workplace the consequences can be very real.

It is not always a familiar person who sexually harasses or attempts to exploit someone sexually at a conference. A Ph.D. student recently told us how she met, at a convention, an admired scholar upon whose work she had based her dissertation. She complimented him on his invited address and enthusiastically discussed her thesis with him. He invited her for a drink to continue the talk, lightly commenting on all the job connections he had and how pleased he would be to help her find employment. He explained that he already had dinner plans, but perhaps she would like to continue their discussion of her career later that evening in his room? Another woman told us a similar story that took place at a sales representatives' convention when she was introduced to a potential client for the materials she promoted. The additional twist for her was that her boss encouraged her to "be nice" to the man, stating that the commissions were well worth a "roll in the hay" with him. She did not oblige. In these cases, the professor, the potential client, and the boss all abused their power.

We do not intend to imply that these are frequent occurrences. Playful flirting is common at conventions, as it is everywhere. We certainly do not want to encourage an oppressive or legalistic atmosphere of suspicion and distrust. Conventions are great places to make contacts, build networks and friendships, and advance your career. We are just suggesting that you be alert to the possibility of the hidden agendas of some conventioneers. Be informed and be prudent.

Summary

Meeting one's social needs and having a good time are legitimate goals at a convention. In addition, social needs overlap with professional needs, for social activities offer valuable opportunities to develop a professional network and establish professional friendships. Convention planners recognize this and often provide social activities and events. Other opportunities are created or taken advantage of by the willing. These can greatly enhance the convention experience. Social hours, dances, sightseeing tours, and hospitality suite events are all good places to mingle with colleagues and, perhaps, find dining or touring companionship. However, any convention activity provides an opportunity to meet people, even paper and poster sessions and business meetings. Indeed, you may begin to consider attending a convention to be like taking a minivacation, where you can benefit both professionally and personally.

8 | Surfing the Exhibits for Products and Publishers

The single best place to be at a convention is the exhibit area. Why? This area can be mutually beneficial to attendees and to the manufacturers and publishers who display their wares. Sometimes complimentary coffee or a no-host snack bar is available to encourage leisurely browsing. We even recall one meeting where a publisher offered complimentary do-it-yourself ice cream sundaes to celebrate the publication of a California author's new text. Ordinarily, a convention just provides food for thought, which is much lower in both fat and calories.

What Exactly Do They Exhibit There?

The size of the exhibit area is generally proportional to the number of attendees at the convention. At the meetings of very large associations, the exhibits often take up the entire main hall of the host city's convention center. There can be hundreds of booths offering the latest products germane to the discipline. In general, these products include books (texts, treatment manuals, professional reviews, and more popularized stories and literary observations), technical equipment (e.g., biofeedback devices, egg-shaped relaxation chairs featuring soothing visual scenes and soft music, special lamps that give off depression-preventing light, computers that will print out what you say aloud to help in note taking and report preparations), informative brochures (e.g., describing residential treatment programs for substance abusers or teenage delinquents), literature produced by national advocacy groups (e.g., those against child abuse and neglect; those for the humane treatment of the mentally ill), and descriptions of the advantages of joining the military service as a way of furthering your professional career. There is something for everyone. If you doubt it, ask any of the representatives working any of the booths.

Companies that make and sell technical equipment related to the discipline rent space in the exhibit area to promote their products and services. Naturally, they display their latest and/or most popular products in competition with everyone else for your attention (and ultimately your dollar or credit card number). The scene is much like an intellectually dignified country fair, without the ferris wheel or animal breeding contests.

This massive array of color, noise, banners, products, customers and browsers, and salespeople can overwhelm the first-time conventioneer who is not expecting such a dazzling display of commercialism at a professional meeting. Luckily, the atmosphere is also very low pressure, so the exhibit area really does offer an excellent and convenient opportunity for attendees to visit the booths, meet people, and learn.

Tip: Visit the exhibits several times—rarely can you see everything in one visit. With each return visit you will feel more comfortable, and very soon you will feel very much at home. (The exhibit area is an excellent place to practice the techniques and strategies of socializing discussed in Chapters 2 and 7.)

Ironically, the exhibit area is often the one area of the convention where admission is carefully monitored, often by uniformed guards. Only those visitors who display official convention badges are permitted to enter, even though the basic purpose of the exhibits is to display and sell items. Those potential customers too poor to register officially (including, of course, the prototypical starving students) cannot enter these hallowed selling grounds. Perhaps convention executives believe that interested nonregistrants are greater risks for robbery. In any case, we recommend that all attendees register officially for the convention, even if it is only to behave in a morally responsible manner. It never hurts to try that approach, even occasionally.

Many exhibitors provide substantial convention discounts if you make purchases on the spot or within a short period following the meeting. Thus, you can save money by patronizing the exhibitors, and you can also learn of any new products or books that have recently become available in your particular interest areas. (We discuss other cost-cutting strategies in Chapter 9.)

Free Stuff

What can you get for free in the exhibit area? A number of vendors hold drawings, often daily, at which they give away some of their products; you enter by leaving your business card. (Of course, as a sophisticated person familiar with the capitalist system, you understand that when you leave your card, it helps these companies generate their mailing lists. As long as this reciprocity is understood, the exchange seems fair.)

The exhibit area usually has several "free—take one" booths. The price is right, of course, but why take a lot of literature to lug around that you really have no interest in? On the other hand, the free brochures may announce upcoming conferences, often international ones, of which you might ordinarily be unaware. Or they may announce the start-up of new journals about to be published in your area. (**Tip:** Your chances of having an article accepted in a brand-new journal may be a little bit better than your having it accepted in a well-known, long-established journal, because the new one will have fewer manuscripts to choose from as it gears up for publication. Of course, a low-quality manuscript will not be accepted at even a fledgling journal—unless you are already very famous in the field.)

You can obtain free textbooks (the accepted vocabulary in this professional context is *complimentary desk copies*) for you to consider for college courses that you are teaching or will be teaching soon. Because this is a very expensive service provided by publishers, it usually is necessary for you to attest or document that you are indeed a faculty member assigned to teach that course. It would be unethical to lie to publishers as a devious method of building your personal library.

Some highly technical books are classified as "professional books," not textbooks suitable for large undergraduate classes. Such books may not be offered as complimentary review copies, but rather may be sent to you "on approval." After 30 to 60 days, you may keep the book for free *if* your college bookstore places at least a minimum order for the book. Otherwise, you will be sent an invoice for it, although an "educational discount" might be included.

Finally, need we remind you that the opportunity to learn and to meet new people (salespeople and fellow conventioneers) at the exhibits is free? Don't limit yourself to thinking that the free benefits there are only tangible ones. **Tip:** If you are one of the exhibiting publishing companies' authors, or a genuine prospective author, there really could be a free lunch for you at the convention! (Some aphorisms are not entirely true.)

Reviewing and Writing

The contacts you make with sales personnel and editors of publishing companies in the exhibits area can be valuable if you are interested in reviewing book manuscripts or preparing your own manuscripts that someone else will review. Publishers maintain lists of instructors in the various subfields of each

EXHIBIT AREA

SAGE PUBLISHING

NEW REVISED ED

D. KELLEHER

" SO MANY BOOKS, SO LITTLE TIME... "

discipline who are capable of providing critical reviews and suggestions for manuscripts of new texts they are developing. While chatting with a publishing company's exhibit booth personnel, you can mention your interest in performing this function. Reviewing is an excellent way to establish a reputation with a company and to display your own writing skills. A second benefit is that you should receive some financial compensation for your work, which indeed is a genuine professional consulting function. **Tip:** The pay for this work, however, is typically rather low for the time required to perform the requested task competently. However, as you do more work for a publisher, or if you present your own book proposal at some later point, you may be able to drive a bit better bargain with that company in the next contract negotiation.

Editors and the sales personnel at publishers' exhibit booths (these may or may not be the same persons) will usually be eager to discuss with you your book writing plans. Although it is certainly not required, it is usually most helpful if you have established something of a track record through previous publications in the field before you propose a major writing project. Putting it another way, landing book contracts following discussions at publishers' convention exhibit booths is much more probable for the more senior members of the discipline than for advanced graduate students or beginning professionals. There are exceptions, of course, but we would advise you to begin this literary trek via the manuscript review process.

Unless you are an indisputable "name" in the field, your previous writing of scientific or professional journal articles will not ordinarily impress publishing house editors much beyond enhancing your professional credibility (which, of course, can certainly be a good idea). Technical writing styles are not sought for texts or popular trade books. Some authors can write well in either format, but others have difficulty translating their work into an easy-reading jargon-free style. Editors want you to be knowledgeable in your field, to be able to write in a way that is appealing and comprehensible to the intended audience (e.g., undergraduate students), and to be able to meet writing deadlines. If you can do that, they do not care much whether you are pretty, bisexual, or wear a beanie with a propeller at lunch.

Are you competent, responsible, and reliable as a writer? If so, and if you would enjoy reviewing or writing in your discipline, get on down to the exhibit area and meet the editors. (Some of them are even nice people and fun to work with, but we are closely guarding those few names.)

We have heard comments from some seasoned conventiongoers to the effect that "there is nothing new" or "the field is stagnating." Even though we are inclined to dispute even the premise of such remarks, we urge such cynics to attend a convention and to *participate* by presenting on the program. See

Chapters 1, 2, and 11 for discussions of the kinds of fears some professionals have about presenting their work in public and handling any critiques or questions extemporaneously. The exhibits offer a large world of opportunities for you to contribute to your discipline by reviewing manuscripts or by proposing and then writing your own professional books.

Summary

To review, we suggest that you spend considerable time in the exhibits area of the convention, whenever you have a break in your daily schedule of seeing posters and listening to papers. By visiting the exhibits, you can

1. maintain currency in your field,
2. become intellectually stimulated by browsing the booths and talking to fellow professionals,
3. learn of the new books and products being marketed in your field,
4. establish personal contacts with publishing house personnel so that you can review manuscripts for them and discuss your own writing plans, and
5. practice assertiveness and social skills with fellow conventioneers.

The exhibit area is a great place to meet old (and young) friends and prospective professional colleagues.

9 | Money Matters and Traveling Smart

There is no free convention lunch. In the "old days," there were enough free hors d'oeuvres and complimentary cocktail parties for attendees practically to subsist without any funds. But due to downturns in the economy in recent years and publishing house budgets being consumed by gigantic book advances given to criminal defendants and politicians (sometimes the same group), such freebies have virtually become extinct. There are certain exceptions for wealthier organizations, such as pharmaceutical company-sponsored medical meetings and conventions of romance novelists.

Attending a professional convention nowadays does cost some money. The good news is that your expenses will most likely be tax deductible (consult your accountant for verification, but that itself could cost you money). It is true that individuals can attend most events at most large professional conventions without registering and thereby avoid paying registration fees. For moral and ethical reasons, however, we recommend that you pay the appropriate registration fee. As a practical matter, a paid fee garners you a name badge to display, which, in turn, could be your key to opportunities for major social and career contacts.

The registration fee for students is nearly always less than that for regular members of the association, and nonmembers are nearly always charged the highest fee. Thus, if you identify with your discipline, it is professionally appropriate and financially advantageous for you to join its association. Paying the registration fee supports the association and only partially defrays the costs of putting on the convention (renting space at the hotel or convention center, printing the program, and other related expenses). Those who do not register are taking advantage and increasing the burden of the friends and colleagues who have done so. Please register officially.

Aside from the necessary registration costs, we offer suggestions in this chapter that are guaranteed to save you money, both in traveling to the convention and in your time there. Cities vary in their expensiveness for tourists and conventioneers. For example, visiting New York City is definitely more expensive than going to Las Vegas or Miami. The greater the daily cost of living in a given city, the more important it is that you utilize strategies to reduce your expenses. We would hope that financial considerations will not prevent you from attending your association's convention, recognizing that there necessarily will be *some* expense involved.

Travel

The cheapest way to travel to a convention is to walk or ride a bicycle. Ordinarily, however, the convention will be in a city at a considerable distance from your home, and such healthful modes of transportation will take too much time. If the convention site is within reasonable driving distance, carpooling is the most economical method of travel. This also provides for built-in social companionship during the trip and later at the meeting itself. You are not likely to be lonely if you arrive with a group, but then you may also have less incentive to meet new people.

The disadvantage of going to a convention with a group of friends is that it can be a definite impediment to your getting the most out of your trip. Regardless of how much you enjoy these folks at home, remember that you can always see them there. Your focus at the meeting should be to expand your social contacts and to pursue professional interests and goals not ordinarily available to you. Returning home in the car pool, you will have the opportunity to catch up with your friends and exchange convention success stories.

Preparation and *planning,* as always, are the best strategies. If you will be traveling alone and by air, usually you can take advantage of airfare sales, and meet all those pesky restrictions, if you plan the trip sufficiently in advance. Of course, the most economical way to fly is to use a complimentary ticket, such as you might be awarded after having been bumped from some previous flight, or to obtain a voucher for a free flight from a frequent flyer club. For example, experienced travelers can become quite skilled at making reservations on typically busy flights that have the maximum probability the planes will be overbooked. When more passengers with reservations show up than the carrier's computers predicted, the airline seeks volunteers to give up their seats in exchange for a future free flight. Volunteering to be bumped can result in some smooth soaring later. This technique is definitely a long-term strategy for getting free air travel to a meeting, but when it works, it can be especially rewarding. One of us (LRF) successfully applied this technique to obtain a round-trip flight between San Diego and Toronto, including airport taxes, for a net cost of $19—for *two.*

Volunteering to give up your seat on an overbooked flight, of course, must be done in advance (anytime up to a year) of the time you will need to travel to your convention. At the time you are bumped, you must also have the extra time available to take another flight to your destination. Sometimes that flight might not be until the next morning, although the airlines will tell you when the next flight is scheduled and the exact amount of reimbursement you can expect for your inconvenience in volunteering. Some carriers will instead give you a voucher to be applied to any future ticket purchase. The amount can vary, but usually you can expect around $300. Others will provide you with a certificate for a round-trip flight to anywhere they fly within the continental United States.

The price of your original ticket, even if it was free, or the distance of your original itinerary does not matter when you become entitled to a free ticket or voucher after you have volunteered to be bumped. If the airline cannot recruit enough volunteers with its first offer, it will often sweeten the incentive by adding value to the voucher or providing complimentary meals, hotel lodging, or a visit to the airline's private membership lounge. Of course, it is a genuine gamble to wait for the ante to be raised, because enough volunteers usually respond to the first call.

Tip: When the airport lounge seems very crowded and it is a popular time to travel, volunteer to give up your seat *before* any announcement is made. Airline clerks are usually appreciative of this and will begin creating a list of volunteers even prior to a definite need for names. Popular travel times are immediately prior to and following major holidays and Friday and Sunday early evenings.

Advance planning and close monitoring of airfares with the help of a travel agent who really does work for you (beyond merely writing out your ticket) can save you hundreds of dollars. Some airlines, such as Southwest, offer two-for-one or "friends fly free" programs. You and a friend (or even a nodding acquaintance) can coordinate your travel to the convention and take advantage of such a program, effectively cutting the cost of your ticket in half. Other airlines, travel clubs, credit card companies, specialty magazines on best airfares, and banks periodically publicize promotions for free or reduced-cost companion airfares. Read the ads and stay alert for special deals that you can use for your convention travel. You really can save significant amounts of money.

If you must make your flight reservation relatively late or the above techniques will not work for you on a particular trip, at least use the convention code number for the "official" airline named for that meeting. Most conferences and professional associations arrange special fares with one or two airlines just for those meetings. At the very least, you will save 5% off the lowest fare otherwise available.

Lodging

The key concept to remember for saving money on hotel costs is *sharing*. Splitting room costs with compatible friends is an excellent way to save. We have known graduate students who have rented a single hotel room and then divided the costs with seven friends, some of whom get beds and some of whom get floor space for sleeping bags. Everyone gets to use the TV and the bathroom and enjoy the heat or air conditioning. Note that hotel management personnel ordinarily do not care for this plan and may even have rules against it. We, of course, do not want to recommend anything illegal, but we wanted to share this tale of successful housing expense reduction.

Tip: Certain discount dining and lodging publications offer very substantial price reductions, such as 50% off hotel rooms. Probably the best is the Entertainment book, which is published in regional editions for most major U.S. cities. It is of great value and you can easily recoup the cost of the book in one night's hotel stay. If you plan to spend sufficient time in an area, you can purchase the edition for that area ahead of time.

However, even if the convention hotel is listed in the Entertainment book, it is unlikely that rooms will be available at the standard 50% discount (because conventioneers will already have reserved most or all of the rooms). The rules of the program also often require that you make hotel reservations within 30 days of your visit, *if* there is space.

With a little planning and research of the area, you probably will be able to discover another motel or hotel very near the convention hotel or convention center for which you can use the Entertainment book discount. You may be in a slightly less luxurious hotel, but not necessarily. In any case, your costs will definitely be very substantially reduced.

There are many good reasons for you to stay in or near the convention hotel. For example, staying nearby means you will be able to attend evening events with convenience. You can take a rest for an hour or so during a busy and tiring day if your room is handy rather than across town. You will not have to carry your own poster materials or copies of papers around with you all day long. You won't need to be loaded down with outdoor clothes for inclement weather while attending sessions. Your convenience and comfort are enhanced, leaving you more time and energy to enjoy the meeting. These seemingly simple benefits go an extraordinarily long way toward helping you get the most out of the presentations and the overall convention. Taking that short siesta in the afternoon can add immeasurably to your fresh and lively participation in the second half of the day's activities.

Tip: Do not give in to pressures from relatives or the lure of false economizing and stay with "Aunt Mary" or "Cousin Billy" while in or near their home city. This is a very common and major error. When you stay with relatives or friends, your attention is taken away from the meeting and its professional and social opportunities. You feel obligated to spend extra time with your hosts and engage in activities that may not even interest you very much (which is likely why you haven't seen these people for such a long time anyway). If you must see relatives or friends in the convention city, or if you even actually want to, schedule visits for either before or after the formal convention. Stay in or near the convention hotel during the meeting.

Eating

We have discussed how to find dinner companions in Chapter 7. Once you have found them, or even if you prefer to dine alone, the questions become, Where do you go to eat? How can you save money?

The Entertainment book and its dining promotion publications are also useful for their many coupons for "2 for 1" dinners or 50% off entrées when dining alone. Of course, you will have to obtain the Entertainment edition for the city you are visiting. Participating restaurants range from the most expensive and elegant to fast-food chains. You can quickly save the cost of the book by using it for two or three meals.

Usually the registration area of the convention includes a table staffed by a local person knowledgeable about and helpful in locating desirable restaurants or particular kinds of cuisine in that city. Sometimes their services include discount coupons for restaurants, shows, or other local attractions. The hotel concierge can also be very helpful in recommending restaurants or other needed services, even if you are not staying in the hotel. The concierge desk is less likely to have discounts available, but it is assertive at least to ask about them.

Room service in your hotel can be another attractive option for meals. It could be a very nice treat, if you are extremely tired, if you just do not happen to want to socialize that evening, if you usually have to prepare your own meals, or if you want to kick back, relax, and spend a romantic evening with a friend. Room service menus are usually more limited than those in the hotel restaurant, and the selections are slightly more expensive. And, of course, the person who delivers room service expects a reasonable tip. (**Tip:** With room service, a fixed-percentage tip may be included in the bill. Be sure to check—it is fiscally foolish to add a gratuity to a gratuity.) The major disadvantage of using room service is that the food usually takes a little longer to arrive than it would in a restaurant, and items designed to be hot may be cool.

Within the confines of convenience, you can save on your food expenses by bringing along fruit, snacks, and beverages from home. Many motels and hotels feature complimentary coffee in their rooms. Others offer inexpensive or free continental breakfasts.

In keeping with our goals of health promotion and convention survival, we proffer our final suggestion on this topic: Save money by eating less. Who among us would not be healthier if we were a few pounds lighter?

If you are independently wealthy, you probably will not be reading this section on how to save money while dining nutritiously. Perhaps you have won your state's lottery since purchasing this book. For everyone else, especially inexperienced travelers, we feel obliged to warn you of the seductive minibars located in most rooms of luxury hotels. These small refrigerators look like personal safes and feature a wide variety of alcoholic and nonalcoholic beverages, nuts, and candy. The reason these appliances look like safes is that they hold cold food items equivalent in value (by the estimate of the hotel management) to the current market value of gold and other precious metals! **Tip:** Bring drinks and snacks along from home or leave the room to obtain them. Even the lobby gift shop or the vending machines in the hotel halls will be comparative bargains relative to the minibar in your room. All hotels offer unlimited free ice.

Dress

Cities in the United States vary significantly in formality. When attending meetings in relatively formal cities, such as New York or Boston, most of the attendees will dress less casually than they might in other cities. Of course, conventions have no formal dress codes. It is not unusual to see someone dressed in shorts and sandals seated next to someone in a dress suit and heels. For those making presentations, the usual expectation is that they will dress more formally than those who are not (unless the meeting is in Hawaii, Miami, or any of the Caribbean islands).

Generally, we recommend packing light and choosing pieces that can be readily mixed and matched. Ease of hand laundering can be an important consideration in maximizing your use of clothes for more occasions. Most new convention attendees tend to bring far too many clothes and end up taking home much of their wardrobe unworn. (**Tip:** There is no need to bring along a heavy iron for pressing clothes. Hotels will provide guests with irons for no charge—just the price of a tip.)

Although traveling can often be expensive, your convention travel costs and daily living expenses can be reduced to much less than you might expect. The advantages of attending your profession's annual convention far outweigh the financial costs. The money you do spend should be documented and brought to the attention of the Internal Revenue Service before April 15 of the following year.

More Money Matters

Some universities will "support" (read "provide some money to") graduate students and faculty members who simply attend a professional meeting. In some cases the support is restricted to those who make formal presentations on the program. Check with your dean or department chair for details, and the earlier, the better. Often a department's travel funds run out early.

There is no need to suffer in order to save money while attending a professional convention. Our suggestions are designed to encourage you to go to the meeting and not be deterred by financial constraints. You are the best judge of your own bank account and your lifestyle needs. If you are accustomed to having an imported bottle of French cabernet sauvignon with dinner each evening, you will be able to continue that tradition while at the convention. If it is more important to mix your own Crystal Light powdered lemonade and save that $80 for another purpose, hotels offer plenty of tap water and complimentary ice. Eat, drink, and be solvent!

Summary

Certainly it will usually cost you some money to travel to your professional convention and to live and eat there for several days. Some of your expenses may be reimbursable and tax deductible. Be sure to save all original receipts pertinent to your travel and living expenses at the convention. A copy of the program, if you presented at the meeting, and your registration badge will also serve as excellent documentation for the IRS.

The privileged few who hold large grants or who are renowned speakers especially invited to the meeting will not need to concern themselves with the associated hotel, restaurant, and transportation costs. Most of us, however, can benefit from all the above-suggested cost-saving strategies. We are pleased to share them with you.

10 | Communicating and Getting Involved

Expanding Your Professional Networks

Communicating, networking, and expanding your professional involvements have been our ongoing, underlying themes throughout this book. All of these are themselves central goals and benefits of attending professional conferences. They can also be methods for achieving your convention goals.

There are a number of tricks of the trade that will facilitate your finding specific people, making contact with them (without endlessly playing computer or telephone tag), and expanding your professional network. These involve negotiating the various communication systems available and adding a few of your own. We address them in this chapter in the hope that you can avoid a lengthy, time-consuming, and inefficient trial-and-error approach to learning how to navigate the communication systems and expand your professional network.

Official Communication Systems and Beyond

Most conventions and conferences have some official way to facilitate attendees' locating and contacting one another. The larger the convention, the more complex the system. At relatively small, intimate meetings, such as those on special topics within specializations within disciplines, making contact is easy. You all gather together, most people stay at the same hotel, and programs often list the names of all people attending. Similarly, events not in the program are easily publicized through fliers and postings and word of mouth, as are special interests anyone might want to promote (e.g., a conference organized by a local institution or a new book).

Finding Out Who Is Attending and Where They Are Staying

At large conferences, finding someone who is in attendance can require a considerable degree of ingenuity. First, you need to know whom you want to contact. This may seem self-evident, but the people with whom you want to get in touch may not be self-evident to you. It is likely there will be a number of people you know beforehand you would like to see if they are attending the convention, but there is also the question, Who just might be at the convention whom I would like to run into? In other words, who are the people you might not immediately think of, but you would like to see if they are around?

Reading through every name in the convention program is tiresome and not foolproof. It is easier to skim the participant index, A through Z, than to read the names in every session. The problem is that people who are not listed in the program frequently attend conventions, but if your target person's name is not in the index of participants, there is nothing more you can do than hang around the halls and keep your eyes open.

Once you know whom you want to see, the process of contacting him or her begins. If the person is in the program, you can always show up at his or her presentation. Usually it is best to try to talk with a presenter after the session rather than before, when he or she may be in a rush and feeling anxious about the impending talk (if he or she has not obtained the benefits of reading our Chapter 11, on reducing convention anxieties).

All you need do is exchange a few words about getting to-gether—quickly setting a time and place would be the ideal. This method may not be convenient to your schedule, how-ever, and if the person is presenting late in the convention, there may be little time left to meet. What next?

Most large conventions have official locator systems from which you can get the names of the hotels or the addresses and phone numbers of where attendees are residing during the con-vention (individuals must give permission for this information to be listed; most do). Now it gets easier. Get the information on the person you want to contact from the locator system, and call his or her hotel. As people generally spend little time in their hotel rooms during conventions (unless they are procras-tinators who are still writing their papers), leave a message that includes your phone number and the times you can be reached (e.g., how late). If the person you're contacting is someone you know, you might want to mention where you will be at certain times or social hours you will be attending. Short of attending their presentations or some other events you know they will attend (e.g., the business meetings for officers of particular spe-cial interest groups), we believe that calling other attendees at their hotels is the most reliable way of making contact. Hotel operators are historically mediocre message takers (we have gotten 6-digit phone numbers to return calls), but now many hotel message systems permit you to leave your own complete voice message.

Convention Message Systems

Some large conventions have official message systems. The oldest and most common is the manual message system. That is, you handwrite messages and leave them, alphabetically by last name, in a central location (or, using carbons, in several locations), so people can skim through the many messages and see if there are any for them. (They can also read all the other messages for people whose last names start with the same let-ter as their own. This system allows for inadvertent invasions of privacy, including the reading by strangers of some "interesting" messages of scheduled social rendezvous not intended for widespread reading.) (**Tip:** Be careful what you write in a message to be delivered in this way!)

More and more, message systems have moved into the technological world and are mediated by computers. The system used at the American Psychological Association's annual conventions is a good example of how the computerized format works. When you register, you get a plastic computer card. When you insert this card into a slot on one of the many computer terminals situated at various locations, you can (a) type in a name and get the person's location during the convention (if that person has registered), and (b) request any messages that might have been left for you. To leave messages, however, you have to go to a desk, show your registration badge (only registered people can leave messages), and dictate your message to someone who will type it in. (Although the technology is available that would allow you to type in your own message with privacy, apparently convention organizers think, and rightly so, we would imagine, that this system protects people from obscene or threatening communications.) Then, when (and if) the person you left a message for checks the monitor for messages, voilà, there it will be.

Certainly, not all conventions have moved to such systems yet. You will have to check out the methods available at the one you are attending (look in the program and ask questions). We have come a long way from the simple procedure of tacking handwritten notes on bulletin boards. (Actually, such bulletin boards were quite versatile, as you could leave messages for anyone who might be interested in them, e.g., "Anyone driving to Houston after the convention?")

In our experience, however, the technologically advanced system used by the APA has many problems as well as advantages. For example, most people don't check their messages frequently (particularly if they are not expecting messages). Some people check for messages rarely, if at all. Also, the frequency with which people check for messages can dwindle as the convention proceeds, especially if, after waiting in long and slow lines, they have been repeatedly treated to computer messages along the lines of "Sorry, there are no messages for [your name]." This terse, but accurate, computer message can be a bit embarrassing socially, because others waiting in line behind you can readily see your name and the computer-defined conclusion that "no one wants to communicate with you." Of course, rationally you realize that others have simply not yet tried to reach you or they may not know how to use the system themselves. (**Tip:** Send yourself a welcome message; even include something positive and inspirational!) This is an experience we are both familiar with. And if the lines are long and you have neither the time nor the patience to wait, you are likely to say, "I'll skip it and check back later." Whether or not there is a later can depend on a host of other distractions.

Do use the message system, but do *not* rely on it. If you can find out where a person you want to see is staying, call his or her hotel. If you can stop by the person's presentation, so much the better. *Cover all bases.* When it comes to communicating, redundancy is a positive quality.

Finally, if you really want to connect with particular people at the convention, don't wait until the convention! Contact them beforehand. This is done all the time, and e-mail makes it extra simple. Why take the chance that someone will get your message on the last day of the meeting, if at all, or that you will be playing computer monitor/telephone tag for most of your stay? All it takes is a simple note or telephone message beforehand: "Are you going?" "Where are you staying?" "These are my plans." "I am free at . . . ." "How about dinner on . . . ?" This can save you a lot of disappointment.

Tip: Although it is appropriate for you to contact someone beforehand whom you do not know—for example, to discuss some professional endeavor—unless you have been having an e-mail relationship with that person, you will want to remain a little formal and feel the person out for what kind of time commitment he or she is prepared to make, if any. For example, "I will be attending the ASA convention in New York in August and I see that you are on the program. I would be interested in meeting with you to discuss some issues regarding the dissertation I am writing on . . . . Will you have any available time when we might connect?"

What Else Is Happening?
Going Beyond the Program

The convention program itself is, of course, a form of communication (see Chapter 3). Often programs are so lengthy it is hard to imagine there could be anything missing from them, but there are almost always happenings, organized by various groups, that are not in the program. You can learn about these in two ways: through word of mouth and through fliers. The former requires that you get around, talk to people, and listen (see Chapters 2 and 7). The latter may be inserted with your registration materials or posted in various places. This requires you to keep your eyes open and read postings (which may not always be adjusted for your particular height or eyesight).

We have addressed extraprogram events in Chapters 4 and 7, but we will briefly review a few ideas here. Special interest groups, divisions of the association, as well as unaffiliated groups may hold meetings, discussions, parties, and other events at the convention that are not listed in the formal program. If you are a member of a special interest group, you may read about your group's events in its newsletter. Sometimes announcements are inserted among the registration materials or even mailed to members several days prior to the meeting. Sometimes they are posted, and sometimes there are tables on which people can deposit fliers.

Many conventions have rules requiring official approval of all materials to be posted (e.g., indicated with a stamp of some sort) and unapproved materials are generally taken down by hotel or convention center staff. Keep this in mind should you want to promote some special interest event.

You can also learn about unpublicized events through word of mouth. Some of these are "by invitation," such as publishers' parties. Many of these invitational events graciously welcome guests, so if someone invites you, certainly go along. In order to learn about these events, and to be invited, you will, of course, need to chat with people and ask questions (e.g., "Do you know of anything going on tonight?"). This also applies to gatherings in special interest group suites and informal meetings of people with special interests in common. Go to the "official" (i.e., in the program) events that interest you to learn about "unofficial" activities that may interest you.

Tip: A word of caution—if something looks suspicious or outside of the larger inclusive structure of the convention (e.g., an offer to attend a private film showing at a local address), ask a lot of questions before you attend and, if you choose to go, perhaps it might be wise to go with someone. We have never heard any stories of the sort this suggestion implies, but we would feel negligent if we did not acknowledge the possibility, however remote, that you could come across some questionable invitations and that you should not assume everything that comes your way is aboveboard. As in any social setting, you should be aware of others' nonverbal signals and be clear about the signals you give off.

Getting Involved in
Your Professional Organization

Professional organizations and the special interest groups within them are continually asserting that they need new blood, young people with fresh ideas, people who have not been involved in the past. They often complain that the same "old" people are doing the job, that change is required, and that they need more human resources. Nonetheless, it is often not easy to break into and become involved in these groups. Occasionally, this exclusiveness is intentional, as some people are simply unwilling to move aside for others, and a group can become so "in-group" that others feel unwelcome. And there are always people who use these groups to maintain their sense of self-importance and for whatever power they provide. More often, however, the seeming platitudes about the need for new members are sincere. So, if you are possibly interested, go and mingle!

There are many things you can do to get involved in your professional organization. Often, people become active in their organizations by being all but dragged in by someone they know who has found a role for them. Ask the people you know who are involved in the association what you can do to help. One inquiry is likely to be enough, but if it isn't, keep asking. Join your regional group and the larger association's special interest groups or divisions. It is much easier to get involved initially at this level. This is particularly so at the regional level. And, again, search out people who are involved in these groups and ask what role you can play. At the regional level, attend local meetings.

Newsletters of special interest groups or divisions frequently publish calls for volunteers to staff task forces or committees. Volunteer—and then be sure to follow up if you are not contacted. There are almost always specific contact persons named in newsletter calls for volunteers.

Use your trip to a convention to make contacts and to offer greater involvement in your professional organization. Throughout this book we have been talking about networking and networking strategies. It is through networking that you greatly increase your chances of easy integration into a working group. Attend the business meetings of the groups you are interested in, attend their social hours, and visit their hospitality suites, if they have them. In all these places introduce yourself, ask about the organization, express your desire to get involved, and say something about your particular interests and skills or expertise. Follow up with the people you have discussed this with, either at the convention or after. And if you are having trouble connecting with the right people, use the communication systems discussed above to leave messages for them expressing your interest (e.g., "I am interested in becoming active in the Division on Ecocriticism. I would like to talk to you and get information about the division and how I can become more involved.") Whatever your ambitions, be they to be president of the association or simply to join a compatible working group with interests and goals in common, first get your foot in the door. It is an open door.

A few more points worth remembering: Active participation in your professional association will further enhance your own professional advancement and visibility. Networking is an important vehicle you can use to get involved in your professional organization, and once you are involved, your network will expand tremendously, and continue to do so. Networks create networks. What is more, you will be contributing to a field you know about and care about. That will be appreciated, and that is, in and of itself, gratifying.

International Meetings and Associations

It has become a cliché to say that the world is shrinking, but, metaphorically speaking, it is. This is as evident in the professional disciplines as it is elsewhere. Canadians have always had a visible presence at conventions held by U.S. associations (and vice versa), but in recent years there has been a growing presence of people from all continents at all national conventions, not only in the United States, but throughout the world. There are also increasing numbers of international associations and conventions. These exist within disciplines as well as across disciplines (e.g., the International Association on Victimology).

Few would argue that internationalizing is not a good thing. Indeed, some of us believe it is one of the most exciting changes taking place and essential if our disciplines are to advance and flourish. The need for a global perspective, we think, is self-evident.

Do take advantage of this exciting development. Check out the international associations and conferences in your area of interest. (**Tip:** There are many ways of doing this. International groups and their meetings are often listed in newsletters and association journals, your national associations can provide you with information, and colleagues can keep you informed.) If you have, or can get, the means to do so, we encourage you to submit papers to and attend some international meetings. Learn what your international colleagues are doing, share your work with an international audience, and develop an international network (and, perhaps, the beginning of an international reputation). In all disciplines, international networks are growing.

Compared with attending national conventions, a bit more work and, usually, a lot more planning may be required for you to attend international conventions. You will also need more and earlier preparation. The earlier you make travel reservations, the likelier you are to get good airfares and hotel rates. You will probably need an unexpired passport, and you may need a visa. Before traveling to some countries you may need certain immunizations (check with your physician for medical information, injections, and prescription emergency medications, e.g., to treat diarrhea). Although this is rarely necessary for travel to the larger cities of the world, there are exceptions; you will want to give this some forethought.

You will also have to do some research. What is the weather like where the convention will be held? Are there any cultural dictates regarding clothing and behavior in certain settings that you need to be aware of? Will you need a foreign-language dictionary to get around? Many organizers of international conventions will send you the names of travel agents who officially represent the conventions. Our experience suggests that these vary tremendously in competence and conscientiousness. You might want to use your own. (**Tip:** Pick a travel agent who knows something about the country you are going to.) Of course, during the convention you will want to stay as close to the convention activities as possible, but you will probably also want to build in some time for a little sightseeing and, perhaps, even travel. (**Tip:** Ratings of hotels vary between countries. For example, a three-star hotel in some countries is not nearly as comfortable as a three-star hotel in the United States.)

If you are an experienced traveler, the steps you need to take will be second nature to you. If you are an inexperienced traveler, attending a convention in another country is an excellent (and tax deductible) way to become experienced. The opportunity to visit a foreign country is a bonus that is not insignificant. Professionally and personally, the benefits to you, your work, and your professional development are enormous.

Summary

Communication skills and systems constitute an important element in the achievement of your convention goals. Using them effectively will facilitate your connecting with people you know, meeting people you want to know, and finding out what is happening beyond the formal convention program. Conventions, as well as local meetings, provide opportunities for you to get involved in the association and to expand your professional networks. Finally, networks are not limited to the national level. Much is occurring in the international arena, and there are exciting opportunities to learn about and participate in international associations and conventions and to move toward a more global disciplinary and interdisciplinary perspective.

11 | Accentuating the Positive

Coping With Fears and Getting the
Most Out of the Convention

We hope that the information we have imparted in the preceding chapters has allayed most of your convention fears and pumped some adrenaline into your anticipation of attending a professional convention. Although some individuals may be nonchalant and fearless, most people experience some level of anxiety in new and unfamiliar situations. This feeling varies from person to person, from mild butterflies overpowered by exhilarating excitement, to restless sleep related to some specific event (e.g., giving a paper), to high levels of clinical anxiety. We are all different, and the sources and extent of our anxieties are outcomes of our personal styles, temperaments, and past experiences.

Regardless of our fears and concerns, there is so much to be gained professionally, and so much fun to be had at the same time, that many of us eagerly look forward to the next convention. We think of attending not as a tedious chore, but as a professional perk.

Convention Fears

There are some common sources of fear among persons anticipating attendance at a professional convention. Some fears may simply be related to discomfort with traveling and not specific to the convention itself. For example, many people are afraid of flying. (**Tip:** For this kind of fear, try deep breathing, meditation, or, if necessary, mild tranquilizers under the supervision of a physician, or even behavior therapy, which has an excellent record of success with this type of problem.)

Some people fear leaving their children or elderly parents or their domestic partners. (**Tip:** Before you leave, set a time when you will call home from the convention each evening, and then make sure you call from wherever you are. Elicit a promise from your loved ones that they will leave you a message at your hotel about any change in their schedule. And of course, make sure everyone who is important to you has the address and phone number where you can be reached while you're away.)

Some people fear getting sick in a strange city. (**Tip:** Speak to your doctor before you leave, and make sure you know how to get in touch with her or him should you need to. Take along whatever medication you may need. Remember, there are competent doctors and good hospitals throughout the United States. The staff at your hotel, as well as the convention organizers, will know how to put you in touch with a doctor if you need one.)

In short, do whatever you have to do to reduce your travel-related anxieties, and don't worry about what other people think about the precautions you choose to take. The important thing is to get to the convention. You will get the most out of it when you are as free as possible from external distractions.

Some people fear crowds or fear being alone and lonely, or they fear both. (It is easy to feel lonely in a crowd because of the sense of anonymity.) In these cases, it is important to try to isolate the specific fears and take whatever action is necessary to minimize or rectify the source. Throughout this book, we have talked about ways of meeting people—finding dinner companions and people to talk to. Check back to Chapters 2, 5, and 7 for some ideas. It will not be possible for you to avoid large groups of people at a convention, but you can usually minimize, if not eliminate, the need to be in large crowds. Of course, this may mean you have to sacrifice attending some events, but it may be worthwhile for you to do this. It is certainly preferable to your missing the convention entirely. For example, you can arrive at the convention site before the meeting is scheduled to begin and register early, before the crowds arrive. (The registration desk is usually crowded at the beginning of a convention.) That way you will already feel "at home" in the hotel or convention center and will know your way around to both the meeting rooms and the restrooms. Your comfort level will rise dramatically.

Although there are many excellent reasons to stay at a convention headquarters hotel, and we highly recommend it (see Chapter 9). If avoiding large crowds is a top priority for you, stay at a hotel central to the convention area, but not one that is a headquarters hotel for the convention. Headquarters hotels are always more crowded, as conventioneers who are not guests there will visit for various and sundry reasons. You may also choose to skip the presentations of really hot (that is, popular) speakers in favor of more intimate conversation hours and the like. Poster sessions may or may not be crowded. Those held at 8:00 a.m. (like nearly all 8:00 a.m. events) are not likely to draw a crowd. Poke your head in and see.

Some people are shy and introverted and question the competence of their social skills and, as a result, their ability to maneuver around a convention. If this describes you, take comfort in knowing that there are many other people out there just like you who are hesitant to assert themselves. People of all kinds of temperaments attend conventions, and who would want it any other way? If you have gotten this far in your professional development, it is likely that your social skills are reasonably adequate. What is more, they won't get any better if you avoid professional events like conventions. (See Chapter 2 for more on assertiveness skills.)

Finally, many people fear they will "make a fool of themselves." What this means is that they fear they will do something "stupid," or reveal themselves as "inadequate." This fear is almost always related to some convention assignment or presentation the person must make. The solution to this kind of fear is *preparation*, which we discuss in detail in Chapter 6. This same kind of fear keeps people from asking questions publicly during the formal Q&A sessions at the ends of talks. (**Tip:** Ask your question informally to the speaker during a one-on-one conversation after the session concludes. This could yield even more information from the speaker than he or she might have given before the larger group—and maybe even an invitation to continue talking elsewhere.)

Preparation is the very best way you can assure yourself that you are capable of effectively performing any task you may have at the convention. This is true for paper and poster presentations, delivering task force reports, and disseminating other kinds of information. Preparation is good treatment for performance anxiety.

Some Notes About Presentation Anxiety

Over cocktails during a social hour at an American Psychological Association annual convention, one of the authors (SRZ) got into a candid discussion with several colleagues about the anxiety symptoms we have when presenting papers. All of us were experienced presenters, so we were surprised to learn that we all have some of the same symptoms. Dry mouth is common. The solution: Keep a glass of water with you and do not hesitate to sip during your talk. (**Tip:** Most presentation rooms have pitchers of water and glasses. They may be on the dais or on a table at the back of the room. Check out the room beforehand, and if no water is available, bring your own.) Stomach butterflies can be confronted with appropriate herbal teas. Many in the group said they visit the bathroom immediately prior to their sessions. The point is, many professionals experience varying levels of anxiety. Acknowledge it and do whatever you can to minimize it and deal with it. (**Tip:** We do *not* recommend such negative approaches as avoidance of the presentation or several presession cocktails to "dull the nerves.")

As a result of this conversation at the social hour, we conducted a study on the topic, which we presented at a poster session at a later meeting of this same association (Rosaria Caporrimo, Sue Zalk, Dorothy Cantor, & Martha Carey, 1989). More than 375 presenters at an APA convention filled out questionnaires about a range of variables related to their presenting at the convention. Preparation, or rather lack of preparation, was the best and most consistent predictor of anxiety. The more prepared presenters felt, the less anxiety they reported experiencing.

Some of the more interesting findings of our study indicated relationships among gender, preparation, experience, and symptoms of anxiety. For women, the amount of anxiety reported was negatively related to preparation; that is, the more prepared a woman was, the less anxious she felt. Years of experience presenting papers did not predict reported anxiety by women, only preparation did. For men, however, preparation was related to reported anxiety only for those who were relatively inexperienced at presenting papers. Men who were experienced presenters had less anxiety regardless of how prepared they were.

There was also one curious but interesting finding. The respondents who were most concerned about their appearance during their presentations (e.g., they had brought a special piece of apparel to wear, had their hair cut) were the men who were least prepared. We don't know what to make of this, but it is intriguing. This does not mean that if you give attention to what you are going to wear and how you want to look that you are unprepared. On the contrary, making these decisions and pulling everything together before you leave for the convention may well be an effective technique to reduce another possible source of anxiety.

Eat, Drink, and Be Merry

Eating at a convention is necessary; drinking (alcoholic beverages, that is) is not. Being merry is a hoped-for state. Conventions can and should be fun. They have definitely become so for us. That is why we have been sharing our own experiences and insights into the whole process for well over a decade at our association's large national convention each year. That is also why we have written this book.

We especially want to reach new professionals and advanced graduate students who will soon be entering the profession. Avoiding conventions—and, worse, being unaware of their potential benefits—is a pitfall that has consumed far too many new professionals. We hope to reach them and to encourage them to discover what convention attendance can do for them.

We have discussed fears and anxieties about attending conventions. These fears naturally range from little more than some mild concerns to full-fledged clinical public speaking performance and social phobias. For the extreme forms of these fears, there are very effective professional treatments available. You should know that and avail yourself of this help, as needed. No one need suffer or be inhibited in professional functioning for long anymore. No one need just "tough it out" or stoically confront his or her fears unaided and unprepared. That kind of discomfort is unnecessary and rarely helpful by itself.

There are some very useful things you can do, and those things are relatively easy. So, at the very least, do what you think is most appropriate for your own situation to overcome any fears or hesitancies you have about attending professional meetings. Be honest with yourself about why you have not attended or have not enjoyed past meetings as much as you otherwise might have. That is the first step.

We have tried to persuade you of the multiple professional and personal benefits of attending conventions. Convention experiences can change your career in many desirable ways—through new contacts, new friends, new research collaborators, new ideas, and more.

We have observed many of our own graduate students exhibiting most of the avoidance behaviors we have discussed in this book. We have listened to some of the very transparent reasons they have offered for not attending meetings or for attending 5-day conventions for only a few hours total. Our hope is that through this book we can reach these individuals as well as their academic advisers, who often seem to model those same convention fears themselves.

Conventions truly can be professionally stimulating and simply fun—if you prepare well, if you behave assertively, and if you *go*. We guarantee it! Trust us. We are doctors.

See you at the meeting.

Summary

Many, if not most, people experience at least some degree of anxiety and concern about attending professional conferences. These may range from mild, undefined worries to more extreme fears and inhibitions. For example, some people experience fears associated with travel, or separation, or crowds, or social skills, or performance. There are simple ways of confronting and coping with most such anxieties, and effective treatments are available for the more exaggerated ones.

Conventions are an important and potentially beneficial aspect of your professional life. There is much to be gained professionally from attending conventions, and they also provide opportunities for you to have fun and to travel. Take advantage of these opportunities, learn to cope with your fears, and go!

Index

About the Authors

Louis R. Franzini is Professor of Psychology at San Diego State University, where he has been on the faculty since 1969. He obtained his B.S. in psychology at the University of Pittsburgh (1963), his M.A. in clinical psychology at the University of Toledo (1965), and his Ph.D. in clinical psychology from the University of Pittsburgh (1968). In 1968-1969 he was a Postdoctoral Fellow in Behavior Modification at the State University of New York at Stony Brook. His international experience includes serving as Training Consultant for the U.S. Peace Corps in Jamaica; as Distinguished Exchange Professor of Psychology at Universite Catholique de Louvain, Louvain-la-Neuve, Belgium; and as Senior Lecturer in the School of Accountancy and Business at Nanyang Technological University, Singapore. His very diverse research publications include clinical research studies on behavior therapy techniques, AIDS risk reduction procedures, heteronegativism, and the assessment of the senses of humor of feminist women and international corporate managers. In addition, he has written text chapters on behavior disorders due to brain injuries, physiological dysfunctions and toxins, psychological assessment, behavior therapy, and the fear of AIDS. He is coauthor, with his colleague Dr. John Grossberg, of *Eccentric and Bizarre Behaviors* (1995), a collection of essays on unusual psychological syndromes. His other professional activities include consulting to academic publishers and public speaking on topics such as assertive management techniques and the use of humor in education and in the workplace. Off campus, you are most likely to find him on the tennis courts or performing stand-up comedy when sufficiently encouraged. Some observers have suggested that the comedy and the tennis are now practically indistinguishable.

Sue Rosenberg Zalk is Vice President for Student Affairs and Professor of Psychology in the Ph.D. Program in Social and Personality Psychology and Educational Psychology at the Graduate School of the City University of New York. At the Graduate School, she served for 3 years as the Ombuds Officer and 9 years as the Director of the Center for the Study of Women and Society, an interdisciplinary research institute. She is editor of *Sex Roles: A Journal of Research* and serves on the editorial board of the *Journal of Social Issues*. She is coauthor or editor of three books and two manuals/guides, including *Women's Realities, Women's Choices* (1995) and *Revolutions in Knowledge: Feminism in the Social Sciences* (1992). She is a past president of the Division of Women's Issues of the New York State Psychological Association and Chair of the Task Force on Mentoring of the Division of the Psychology of Women of the American Psychological Association. Her scholarship is in the area of gender roles and attitudes, the psychology of women and gender, and racial prejudice. She has received grants for projects on incorporating scholarship on women of color into the liberal arts curriculum. She is currently engaged in an international project on the working and living environments of poor urban women, and she consults on sexual harassment and gender discrimination in the academy and in the workplace. Her favorite recreational activity is scuba diving.